COMMON CORE

ENGLISH LANGUAGE ARTS

Activities that Captivate, Motivate, & Reinforce

Grade 7

by Jodie Fransen

IncentivePublications

BY WORLD BOOK

a Scott Fetzer company

Illustrated by Kathleen Bullock
Cover by Penny Laporte

Print Edition ISBN 978-1-62950-202-1
E-book Edition ISBN 978-1-62950-203-8 (PDF)

Copyright © 2014 World Book, Inc. All rights reserved. No part of this publication may be reproduced, stored in a retrieval system, or transmitted in any form or by any means (electronic, mechanical, photocopying, recording, or otherwise) without written permission from World Book, Inc./Incentive Publications, with the exception below.

WORLD BOOK is a registered trademark or trademark of World Book, Inc.

Pages labeled with the statement **Copyright © 2014 World Book, Inc./Incentive Publications, Chicago, IL** are intended for reproduction. Permission is hereby granted to the purchaser of one copy of **COMMON CORE ENGLISH LANGUAGE ARTS GRADE 7** to reproduce these pages in sufficient quantities only for meeting the purchaser's own noncommercial educational needs.

Several passages in this book are borrowed or adapted from these Incentive Publications products: *Basic Not Boring Reading Comprehension, Middle Grades; Basic Not Boring Writing, Middle Grades; Puzzle It! Language Puzzles; Use It Don't Lose It: Daily Language Practice, Grade 7; I've Got It! Reading and Literature Skills;* and *If You're Trying to Get Better Grades Language Arts, Middle Grades.* Other sources cited or consulted are noted on individual pages, accompanying the passages.

World Book, Inc.
233 North Michigan Avenue
Suite 2000
Chicago, Illinois, 60601 U.S.A.

For information about World Book and Incentive Publications products, call **1-800-967-5325,** or visit our websites at **www.worldbook.com** and **www.incentivepublications.com.**

Printed in the United States by Sheridan Books, Inc.
Chelsea, Michigan
1st Printing March 2014

CONTENTS

Great Support for
Common Core State Standards!

Invite your students to join in on adventures and mysteries with colorful
characters. The high-appeal topics and illustrations will spark their
interest as they

> . . . ponder how to respond to a churlish shark,
>
> . . . take daring leaps with a world-class bungee jumper,
>
> . . . help detectives track down international smugglers,
>
> . . . listen in on some curious (and tasty) court cases,
>
> . . . learn how to make a mummy,
>
> . . . visit an entire harbor filled with molasses,
>
> . . . get a lesson from a talking pencil,
>
> . . . explore mysteries of the Abominable Snowman and the lost empire of Atlantis,
>
> . . . watch an adventurer hitchhike with a refrigerator around an entire country,
>
> . . . discover how potato chips, Coca-Cola®, and chocolate chip cookies were invented by accident,
>
> . . . and tackle many other engaging ventures.

And while they follow these escapades, they will be moving toward competence in critical language
skills that they need for success in the real world.

How to Use This Book

- The pages are tools to support your teaching of the concepts, processes, and skills outlined in the
Common Core State Standards. This is not a curriculum; it is a collection of intriguing experiences to
use as you work with your students or children.

- Use any given page to introduce, explain, teach, practice, extend, assess, provide independent work
for, start a discussion about, or get students collaborating on a standard, skill, or concept.

- Use any page in a large-group or small-group setting to deepen understandings and expand
knowledge and skills.

- Pages are **not** intended for use solely as independent work. Do the activities together or review and
discuss the work together.

- Each activity is focused on a particular standard or cluster of standards. However, most pages use or
can be expanded to strengthen other standards as well.

- The book is organized according to the Common Core language strands. Use the tables on pages 9
to 19, the page labels, and notations on the Contents pages to identify the standards supported by
each page.

- For further mastery of Common Core State Standards, see the suggestions on page 8.

About Common Core English Language Arts Standards

The Common Core State Standards for English Language Arts at the middle-grades level aim to build strong content knowledge across a wide range of subject areas. They are also designed to develop capabilities for thoughtful use of technology and digital media; for finding, applying, and evaluating evidence; for working and thinking independently; and for deepening reasoning and understanding. To best help students gain and master these robust standards for reading, writing, speaking, listening, and language:

1. Know the standards well. Keep them in front of you. Understand for yourself the big picture of what the standards seek to do. (See www.corestandards.org.)

2. Work to apply, expand, and deepen student skills. With activities in this book (or with any other learning activities), plan to include

   . . . collaboration with peers in pairs, small groups, and large groups.

   . . . plenty of discussion and integration of language content.

   . . . emphasis on asking questions, analyzing, careful reading and listening, finding evidence, and reasoning.

   . . . lots of observation, meaningful feedback, follow-up, and reflection.

3. Ask questions that advance reasoning, discernment, relevance, and real-life connection:

- *Why? What does this mean?*
- *How do you know?*
- *What led you to this conclusion?*
- *Where did you find this?*
- *What else do you know (or need to know)?*
- *What is the evidence?*
- *Where else could you look?*
- *How is _____ like (or unlike) _____?*
- *What would another viewpoint be?*
- *What does the text infer?*
- *What is the purpose of the presentation?*
- *What beliefs lie behind the writer's claims? How can you tell?*
- *Do you agree? Why or why not?*
- *How does this part affect that part?*
- *Where have you seen something like this before?*
- *How does the structure of the text affect the message?*

- *What are the parts? How do they work together?*
- *How does the text confirm your ideas?*
- *How would this vary for a different purpose, place, person, or situation?*
- *How does the idea of the text (or speech or argument) build?*
- *How is this idea affected by the ideas that came before it?*
- *How could you write (or say) this to give _____ effect?*
- *What is the effect of using this word (or phrase, or idea, or structure)?*
- *What is the writer's (or speaker's) viewpoint or bias? How can you tell?*
- *So what? (What difference does this information, or perspective, or discovery make?)*

College and Career Readiness Anchor Standards (CCRS)
for Reading, Grades K-12

Anchor Standard	Standard	Pages that Support
Key Ideas and Details		
CCRA.R.1	Read closely to determine what the text says explicitly and to make logical inferences from it; cite specific textual evidence when writing or speaking to support conclusions drawn from the text.	22, 23, 24, 25, 26-27, 30-31, 36, 37, 38, 39, 40-41, 44, 45, 46-47, 48, 50, 54, 55, 56, 57, 58-59, 60-61, 62-63, 64, 82-83
CCRA.R.2	Determine central ideas or themes of a text and analyze their development; summarize the key supporting details and ideas.	25, 26-27, 28, 30-31, 45, 46-47, 48, 49, 56, 58-59, 60-61, 62-63, 64, 84
CCRA.R.3	Analyze how and why individuals, events, and ideas develop and interact over the course of a text.	29, 30-31, 50, 51
Craft and Structure		
CCRA.R.4	Interpret words and phrases as they are used in a text, including determining technical, connotative, and figurative meanings, and analyze how specific word choices shape meaning or tone.	32, 33, 34, 35, 52, 53, 54, 55
CCRA.R.5	Analyze the structure of texts, including how specific sentences, paragraphs, and larger portions of the text (e.g., a section, chapter, scene, or stanza) relate to each other and the whole.	36, 37, 56, 57
CCRA.R.6	Assess how point of view or purpose shapes the content and style of a text.	38, 39, 58, 59
Integration of Knowledge and Ideas		
CCRA.R.7	Integrate and evaluate content presented in diverse media and formats, including visually and quantitatively, as well as in words.	40-41, 64
CCRA.R.8	Delineate and evaluate the argument and specific claims in a text, including the validity of the reasoning as well as the relevance and sufficiency of the evidence.	60-61
CCRA.R.9	Analyze how two or more texts address similar themes or topics in order to build knowledge or to compare the approaches the authors take.	40-41, 42, 62-63
Range of Reading and Level of Text Complexity		
CCRA.R.10	Read and comprehend complex literary and informational texts independently and proficiently.	22-42, 44-64

Copyright © 2014 World Book, Inc./
Incentive Publications, Chicago, IL

Reading Standards for Literature, Grade 7

ELA Standard	Standard	Pages that Support
Key Ideas and Details		
RL7.1	Cite several pieces of textual evidence to support analysis of what the text says explicitly as well as inferences drawn from the text.	22, 23, 24, 25, 26-27, 30-31, 36, 37, 38, 39, 40-41, 82-83
RL7.2	Determine a theme or central idea of a text and analyze its development over the course of the text; provide an objective summary of the text.	25, 26-27, 28, 30-31
RL7.3	Analyze how particular elements of a story or drama interact (e.g., how setting shapes the characters or plot).	29, 30-31
Craft and Structure		
RL7.4	Determine the meaning of words and phrases as they are used in a text, including figurative and connotative meanings; analyze the impact of rhymes and other repetitions of sounds (e.g., alliteration) on a specific verse or stanza of a poem or section of a story or drama.	32, 33, 34, 35
RL7.5	Analyze how a drama's or poem's form or structure (e.g., soliloquy, sonnet) contributes to its meaning.	36, 37, 82-83
RL7.6	Analyze how an author develops and contrasts the points of view of different characters or narrators in a text.	38, 39
Integration of Knowledge and Ideas		
RL7.7	Compare and contrast a written story, drama, or poem to its audio, filmed, staged, or multimedia version, analyzing the effects of techniques unique to each medium (e.g., lighting, sound, color, or camera focus and angles in a film).	42
RL7.8	(Not applicable to literature)	64
RL7.9	Compare and contrast a fictional portrayal of a time, place, or character and a historical account of the same period as a means of understanding how authors of fiction use or alter history.	40-41, 58-59, 62-63
Range of Reading and Level of Text Complexity		
RL6.10	By the end of the year, read and comprehend literature, including stories, dramas, and poems, in the grades 6–8 text complexity band proficiently, with scaffolding as needed at the high end of the range.	22-42

10 Copyright © 2014 World Book, Inc./ Incentive Publications, Chicago, IL

Reading Standards for Informational Text, Grade 7

ELA Standard	Standard	Pages that Support
Key Ideas and Details		
RI.7.1	Cite several pieces of textual evidence to support analysis of what the text says explicitly as well as inferences drawn from the text.	44, 45, 46-47, 48, 50, 54, 55, 56, 57, 58-59, 60-61, 62-63, 64
RI.7.2	Determine two or more central ideas in a text and analyze their development over the course of the text; provide an objective summary of the text.	45, 46-47, 48, 49, 56, 58-59, 60-61, 62-63, 64, 84
RI.7.3	Analyze the interactions between individuals, events, and ideas in a text (e.g., how ideas influence individuals or events, or how individuals influence ideas or events).	50-51
Craft and Structure		
RI.7.4	Determine the meaning of words and phrases as they are used in a text, including figurative, connotative, and technical meanings; analyze the impact of a specific word choice on meaning and tone.	52, 53, 54, 55
RI.7.5	Analyze the structure an author uses to organize a text, including how the major sections contribute to the whole and to the development of the ideas.	56, 57
RI.7.6	Determine an author's point of view or purpose in a text and analyze how the author distinguishes his or her position from that of others.	58, 59
Integration of Knowledge and Ideas		
RI.7.7	Compare and contrast a text to an audio, video, or multimedia version of the text, analyzing each medium's portrayal of the subject (e.g., how the delivery of a speech affects the impact of the words).	64
RI.7.8	Trace and evaluate the argument and specific claims in a text, assessing whether the reasoning is sound and the evidence is relevant and sufficient to support the claims.	60-61
RI.7.9	Analyze how two or more authors writing about the same topic shape their presentations of key information by emphasizing different evidence or advancing different interpretations of facts.	58-59, 62-63

College and Career Readiness Anchor Standards (CCRS)
for Writing, Grades K-12

Anchor Standard	Standard	Pages that Support
Range of Reading and Level of Text Complexity		
RI.7.10	By the end of the year, read and comprehend literary nonfiction in the grades 6–8 text complexity band proficiently, with scaffolding as needed at the high end of the range.	44-64
Text Types and Purposes		
CCRA.W.1	Write arguments to support claims in an analysis of substantive topics or texts, using valid reasoning and relevant and sufficient evidence.	66-68
CCRA.W.2	Write informative/explanatory texts to examine and convey complex ideas and information clearly and accurately through the effective selection, organization, and analysis of content.	69-71
CCRA.W.3	Write narratives to develop real or imagined experiences or events using effective technique, well-chosen details, and well-structured event sequences.	72-74
Production and Distribution of Writing		
CCRA.W.4	Produce clear and coherent writing in which the development, organization, and style are appropriate to task, purpose, and audience.	66-68, 69-71, 72-74, 75, 76-77, 78
CCRA.W.5	Develop and strengthen writing as needed by planning, revising, editing, rewriting, or trying a new approach.	76-77
CCRA.W.6	Use technology, including the Internet, to produce and publish writing and to interact and collaborate with others.	79-81 *See note below.*
Research to Build and Present Knowledge		
CCRA.W.7	Conduct short as well as more sustained research projects based on focused questions, demonstrating understanding of the subject under investigation.	79-81
CCRA.W.8	Gather relevant information from multiple print and digital sources, assess the credibility and accuracy of each source, and integrate the information while avoiding plagiarism.	79-81
CCRA.W.9	Draw evidence from literary or informational texts to support analysis, reflection, and research.	82-83, 84

Standard 6: *Use technology as a part of your approach for any of the activities in this writing section. Students can create, dictate, photograph, scan, enhance with art or color, or share any of the products they create as a part of these pages.*

---

12 Copyright © 2014 World Book, Inc./ Incentive Publications, Chicago, IL

Writing Standards, Grade 7

ELA Standard	Standard	Pages that Support
Range of Writing		
CCRA.W.10	Write routinely over extended time frames (time for research, reflection, and revision) and shorter time frames (a single sitting or a day or two) for a range of tasks, purposes, and audiences.	66-82
Text Types and Purposes		
W.7.1	Write arguments to support claims with clear reasons and relevant evidence.	66-68
W.7.1a	Introduce claim(s), acknowledge alternate or opposing claims, and organize the reasons and evidence logically.	66-68
W.7.1b	Support claim(s) with logical reasoning and relevant evidence, using accurate, credible sources and demonstrating an understanding of the topic or text.	66-68
W.7.1c	Use words, phrases, and clauses to create cohesion and clarify the relationships among claim(s), reasons, and evidence.	66-68
W.7.1d	Establish and maintain a formal style.	66-68
W.7.1e	Provide a concluding statement or section that follows from and supports the argument presented.	66-68
W.7.2	Write informative/explanatory texts to examine a topic and convey ideas, concepts, and information through the selection, organization, and analysis of relevant content.	69-71
W.7.2a	Introduce a topic clearly, previewing what is to follow; organize ideas, concepts, and information, using strategies such as definition, classification, comparison/contrast, and cause/effect; include formatting (e.g., headings), graphics (e.g., charts, tables), and multimedia when useful to aiding comprehension.	69-71
W.7.2b	Develop the topic with relevant facts, definitions, concrete details, quotations, or other information and examples.	69-71
W.7.2c	Use appropriate transitions to create cohesion and clarify the relationships among ideas and concepts.	69-71
W.7.2d	Use precise language and domain-specific vocabulary to inform about or explain the topic.	69-71
W.7.2e	Establish and maintain a formal style.	69-71
W.7.2f	Provide a concluding statement or section that follows from and supports the information or explanation presented.	72-74
W.7.3	Write narratives to develop real or imagined experiences or events using effective technique, descriptive details, and clear event sequences.	72-74

Writing standards continue on next page.

Copyright © 2014 World Book, Inc./
Incentive Publications, Chicago, IL

Common Core Reinforcement Activities — 7th Grade Language

Writing Standards, Grade 7, continued

ELA Standard	Standard	Pages that Support
W.7.3a	Engage and orient the reader by establishing a context and introducing a narrator and/or characters; organize an event sequence that unfolds naturally and logically.	72-74
W.7.3b	Use narrative techniques, such as dialogue, pacing, and description, to develop experiences, events, and/or characters.	72-74
W.7.3c	Use a variety of transition words, phrases, and clauses to convey sequence and signal shifts from one time frame or setting to another.	72-74
W.7.3d	Use precise words and phrases, relevant descriptive details, and sensory language to convey experiences and events.	72-74
W.7.3e	Provide a conclusion that follows from the narrated experiences or events.	72-74
Production and Distribution of Writing		
W.7.4	Produce clear and coherent writing in which the development, organization, and style are appropriate to task, purpose, and audience. (Grade-specific expectations for writing types are defined in standards 1–3 above.)	66-68, 69-71, 72-74, 75, 76-77, 78
W.7.5	With some guidance and support from peers and adults, develop and strengthen writing as needed by planning, revising, editing, rewriting, or trying a new approach, focusing on how well purpose and audience have been addressed. (Editing for conventions should demonstrate command of Language standards 1–3 up to and including grade 7 here.)	76-77
W.7.6	Use technology, including the Internet, to produce and publish writing and link to and cite sources as well as to interact and collaborate with others, including linking to and citing sources.	79-81 *See note below.*
Research to Build and Present Knowledge		
W.7.7	Conduct short research projects to answer a question, drawing on several sources and generating additional related, focused questions for further research and investigation.	79-81
W.7.8	Gather relevant information from multiple print and digital sources, using search terms effectively; assess the credibility and accuracy of each source; and quote or paraphrase the data and conclusions of others while avoiding plagiarism and following a standard format for citation..	79-81
W.7.9	Draw evidence from literary or informational texts to support analysis, reflection, and research.	82-84

Standard 6: *Use technology as a part of your approach for any of the activities in this writing section. Students can create, dictate, photograph, scan, enhance with art or color, or share any of the products they create as a part of these pages.*

Copyright © 2014 World Book, Inc./ Incentive Publications, Chicago, IL

College and Career Readiness Anchor Standards (CCRS) for Speaking and Listening, Grades K-12

Anchor Standard	Standard	Pages that Support
W.7.9a	Apply grade 7 Reading standards to literature (e.g., "Compare and contrast a fictional portrayal of a time, place, or character and a historical account of the same period as a means of understanding how authors of fiction use or alter history").	82-83
W.7.9b	Apply grade 7 Reading standards to literary nonfiction (e.g. "Trace and evaluate the argument and specific claims in a text, assessing whether the reasoning is sound and the evidence is relevant and sufficient to support the claims").	84
Range of Writing		
W.7.10	Write routinely over extended time frames (time for research, reflection, and revision) and shorter time frames (a single sitting or a day or two) for a range of discipline-specific tasks, purposes, and audiences.	66-84
Comprehension and Collaboration		
CCRA.SL.1	Prepare for and participate effectively in a range of conversations and collaborations with diverse partners, building on others' ideas and expressing their own clearly and persuasively.	90-91

Note on range and content of student speaking and listening:

To build a foundation for college and career readiness, students must have ample opportunities to take part in a variety of rich, structured conversations—as part of a whole class, in small groups, and with a partner. Being productive members of these conversations requires that students contribute accurate, relevant information; respond to and develop what others have said; make comparisons and contrasts; and analyze and synthesize a multitude of ideas in various domains.

New technologies have broadened and expanded the role that speaking and listening play in acquiring and sharing knowledge and have tightened their link to other forms of communication. Digital texts confront students with the potential for continually updated content and dynamically changing combinations of words, graphics, images, hyperlinks, and embedded video and audio.

Speaking and Listening Standards: The speaking and listening standards are not specifically addressed in this book. However, most pages can be used for conversation and collaboration. Teachers and parents are encouraged to use the activities in a sharing and discussion format. Many of the pages include visual information that students can include in the integration and evaluation of information.

In addition, most of the texts and activities can be adapted to listening activities or can be used to support the listening and speaking standards.

Speaking and Listening Standards, Grade 7

ELA Standard	Standard	Pages that Support
CCRA.SL.2	Integrate and evaluate information presented in diverse media and formats, including visually, quantitatively, and orally.	93, 94, 98
CCRA.SL.3	Evaluate a speaker's point of view, reasoning, and use of evidence and rhetoric.	95, 98
Presentation of Knowledge and Ideas		
CCRA.SL.4	Present information, findings, and supporting evidence such that listeners can follow the line of reasoning and the organization, development, and style are appropriate to task, purpose, and audience.	95, 96, 97, 98
CCRA.SL.5	Make strategic use of digital media and visual displays of data to express information and enhance understanding of presentations.	95, 96, 97, 98
CCRA.SL.6	Adapt speech to a variety of contexts and communicative tasks, demonstrating command of formal English when indicated or appropriate.	96, 97
Comprehension and Collaboration		
SL7.1	Engage effectively in a range of collaborative discussions (one-on-one, in groups, and teacher-led) with diverse partners on grade 7 topics, texts, and issues, building on others' ideas and expressing their own clearly.	86-92
SL7.1a	Come to discussions prepared, having read or researched material under study; explicitly draw on that preparation by referring to evidence on the topic, text, or issue to probe and reflect on ideas under discussion.	86, 88
SL7.1b	Follow rules for collegial discussions, track progress toward specific goals and deadlines, and define individual roles as needed.	86, 89
SL7.1c	Pose questions that elicit elaboration and respond to others' questions and comments with relevant observations and ideas that bring the discussion back on topic as needed.	86, 89
SL7.1d	Acknowledge new information expressed by others and, when warranted, modify their own views.	90, 91, 92

Copyright © 2014 World Book, Inc./ Incentive Publications, Chicago, IL

College and Career Readiness Anchor Standards (CCRS)
for Language, Grades K-12

Anchor Standard	Standard	Pages that Support
SL7.2	Analyze the main ideas and supporting details presented in diverse media and formats (e.g., visually, quantitatively, orally) and explain how the ideas clarify a topic, text, or issue under study.	93, 94, 98
SL7.3	Delineate a speaker's argument and specific claims, evaluating the soundness of the reasoning and the relevance and sufficiency of the evidence.	94
Presentation of Knowledge and Ideas		
SL7.4	Present claims and findings, emphasizing salient points in a focused, coherent manner with pertinent descriptions, facts, details, and examples; use appropriate eye contact, adequate volume, and clear pronunciation.	95, 96, 97, 98
SL7.5	Include multimedia components and visual displays in presentations to clarify claims and findings and emphasize salient points.	95, 96, 97, 98
SL7.6	Adapt speech to a variety of contexts and tasks, demonstrating command of formal English when indicated or appropriate. (See grade 7 Language standards 1 and 3 here for specific expectations.)	96, 97
Conventions of Standard English		
CCRA.L.1	Demonstrate command of the conventions of standard English grammar and usage when writing or speaking.	100, 101, 102, 103, 104, 105
CCRA.L.2	Demonstrate command of the conventions of standard English capitalization, punctuation, and spelling when writing.	106, 107, 108, 109

Note on range and content of student language use:

To build a foundation for college and career readiness in language, students must gain control over many conventions of standard English grammar, usage, and mechanics as well as learn other ways to use language to convey meaning effectively. They must also be able to determine or clarify the meaning of grade-appropriate words encountered through listening, reading, and media use; come to appreciate that words have nonliteral meanings, shadings of meaning, and relationships to other words; and expand their vocabulary in the course of studying content. The inclusion of Language standards in their own strand should not be taken as an indication that skills related to conventions, effective language use, and vocabulary are unimportant to reading, writing, speaking, and listening; indeed, they are inseparable from such contexts.

Language Standards, Grade 7

ELA Standard	Standard	Pages that Support
Knowledge of Language		
CCRA.L.3	Apply knowledge of language to understand how language functions in different contexts, to make effective choices for meaning or style, and to comprehend more fully when reading or listening.	110, 111
Vocabulary Acquisition and Use		
CCRA.L.4	Determine or clarify the meaning of unknown and multiple-meaning words and phrases by using context clues, analyzing meaningful word parts, and consulting general and specialized reference materials, as appropriate.	112, 113, 114, 115, 116, 117, 118, 119, 120, 121, 122, 123, 124, 125, 126
CCRA.L.5	Demonstrate understanding of figurative language, word relationships, and nuances in word meanings.	120, 121, 122, 123, 124, 125
CCRA.L.6	Acquire and use accurately a range of general academic and domain-specific words and phrases sufficient for reading, writing, speaking, and listening at the college and career readiness level; demonstrate independence in gathering vocabulary knowledge when encountering an unknown term important to comprehension or expression.	52, 53, 54, 126
Conventions of Standard English		
L.7.1	Demonstrate command of the conventions of standard English grammar and usage when writing or speaking.	100-105
L.7.1a	Explain the function of phrases and clauses in general and their function in specific sentences.	100, 101
L.7.1b	Choose among simple, compound, complex, and compound-complex sentences to signal differing relationships among ideas.	102, 103
L.7.1c	Place phrases and clauses within a sentence, recognizing and correcting misplaced and dangling modifiers.	104, 105
L.7.2	Demonstrate command of the conventions of standard English capitalization, punctuation, and spelling when writing.	106, 107, 108, 109
L.7.2a	Use a comma to separate coordinate adjectives (e.g., *It was a fascinating, enjoyable movie but not He wore an old, green shirt*).	107
L7.2b	Spell correctly.	108-109

Language standards continue on next page.

Copyright © 2014 World Book, Inc./ Incentive Publications, Chicago, IL

Language Standards for Grade 7, continued

ELA Standard	Standard	Pages that Support
Knowledge of Language		
L.7.3	Use knowledge of language and its conventions when writing, speaking, reading, or listening.	100-111
L.7.3a	Choose language that expresses ideas precisely and concisely, recognizing and eliminating wordiness and redundancy.	110, 111
Vocabulary Acquisition and Use		
L.7.4	Determine or clarify the meaning of unknown and multiple-meaning words and phrases based on Grade 7 reading and content, choosing flexibly from a range of strategies.	112-119
L.7.4a	Use context (e.g., the overall meaning of a sentence or paragraph; a word's position or function in a sentence) as a clue to the meaning of a word or phrase.	112, 113, 114
L.7.4b	Use common, grade-appropriate Greek or Latin affixes and roots as clues to the meaning of a word (e.g., *belligerent, bellicose, rebel*).	115, 116
L.7.4c	Consult general and specialized reference materials (e.g., dictionaries, glossaries, thesauruses), both print and digital, to find the pronunciation of a word or determine or clarify its precise meaning or its part of speech.	117, 118
L.7.4d	Verify the preliminary determination of the meaning of a word or phrase (e.g., by checking the inferred meaning in context or in a dictionary).	119
L.7.5	Demonstrate understanding of figurative language, word relationships, and nuances in word meanings.	120-125
L.7.5a	Interpret figures of speech (e.g., literary, biblical, and mythological allusions) in context.	120, 121
L.7.5b	Use the relationship between particular words (e.g., synonym/antonym, analogy) to better understand each of the words.	122, 123
L.7.5c	Distinguish among the connotations (associations) of words with similar denotations (definitions) (e.g., *refined, respectful, polite, diplomatic, condescending*).	124, 125
L.7.6	Acquire and use accurately grade-appropriate general academic and domain-specific words and phrases; gather vocabulary knowledge when considering a word or phrase important to comprehension or expression.	52, 53, 54, 126

READING

LITERATURE

Grade 7

TEXT DETECTING

Every good reader examines text closely and follows clues to understand what the writer is saying explicitly as well as what ideas or messages may be implied. Put your best detecting skills to work every time you read.

Gotcha!

Up a long, rickety staircase
Behind a creaking, rusty-hinged door
In a dark and musty attic space
Cramped by cast-off objects
strangled by cobwebs
And obscured by decades of dust,
BLOOD
Stained a rough-hewn floor where,
long ago,
A murder had taken place—
A murder for which
The villain has never paid his debt.
An amateur sleuth
And an aspiring coroner
Could detect
That the blood was human,
But of the mutilated body,
Only three legs
Were left intact.

Read "Gotcha" and answer the questions.

1. What has the writer explicitly stated to tell the reader what is happening?

2. What has the writer inferred or left for the reader to figure out?

3. Who is the victim of the poem? What specific words or phrases in the poem led you to this conclusion?

4. How did the writer set you up to anticipate a certain sequence of events?

5. How did the writer surprise you?

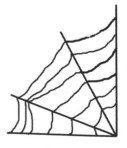

Name

Copyright © 2014 World Book, Inc./ Incentive Publications, Chicago, IL

EYES OF THE NIGHT

Someone is watching. Clues in the passage will help you figure out who it is!

Read the text closely and answer the questions. Be prepared to cite evidence from the text to defend your answers.

I see her every night—sleek, with orange and black stripes bleeding into the shadowy darkness. She slinks, a graceful predator stealing on silent paws—appearing and disappearing in the blink of an eye.

I've watched her grow from a furry cub to a lean, independent warrior—just as I watched generations before her. But there is a change in the landscape. The abundance of wildlife is shrinking. Villages and towns have sprawled into chaotic cities. With each of my nightly rotations, the electric lights multiply.

She can sense it. Her ears are back. Her eyes dart nervously, searching for signs of the human intruders. Her nightly food forays are longer. Often she is still hungry at dawn. From all sides, the lights creep closer and closer to her domain.

When will the humans decide that their cities are large enough? Will they stop in time? I hold my breath with this fragile hope. I cannot imagine my nightly passage without these glimpses of her beauty.

1. Who is the narrator? How do you know?

2. Why is the phrase "…just as I watched generations before her" important in this passage?

3. What specifically is the narrator watching? Which words give it away?

4. What is it that worries the narrator? How can you tell?

5. What words does the writer use to show her personal convictions?

Name

ENCOUNTER WITH A MYTH

Has Lucas encountered a myth? Or is it real?

Read his letter. Then answer the questions below. Be prepared to point to specific things in the letter to defend your answers in a discussion with classmates.

June 24
Castletown, Isle of Man

Dear Jadyn,

The story I am about to tell you is true. I'm sharing it with you because I know you are the one friend who will believe me. My trip to the British Isles has been fantastic. I'll fill you in on all the amazing sights and adventures when I get home. But this one can't wait. I must confess that folklore has always intrigued me, and the traditions regarding mermaids are no exception. But I thought the tales were myths.

On a boat trip to the Isle of Man yesterday, a silvery tail splashed above the surface alongside the boat. Passengers waved their arms excitedly—astonished at the size of the glistening fish. Repeatedly, the fish waved its tail as it followed our craft. We pointed and cheered. It was not long before the excitement turned to gasps and squeals as we caught sight of long, flowing red hair. And when the slim female form of a slender back blending into the shimmering tail surfaced, all utterances stopped. We froze in silence—the shock so paralyzing that no one even thought to click the cameras we held in our hands. There was no mistake. We all saw her.

She did not appear again. No one captured an image, but all passengers agree on what we saw. We finished the trip awestruck, speaking in low, reverent tones. There's nothing more to say. I can only tell you that I am certain of what I saw and honored that she chose to reveal herself.

Your friend,
Lucas

1. What effect does the first sentence have on the tone of the story?

2. How does the writer first put the idea of mermaids into the reader's mind?

3. What evidence does the writer use to support his belief in mermaids?

4. Do you believe he actually saw a mermaid? Why or why not?

Name

Copyright © 2014 World Book, Inc./
Incentive Publications, Chicago, IL

A CASE OF FAUX PASTRIES

Something is awry in Cream Puff Heaven. With sharp reading, you'll be able to evaluate this strange case.

The theme of a story is its central idea. It can be directly stated or implied. Read *Case #215* to determine its theme.

Case #215: Claire v. Cream Puff Heaven

Judge Leslie DeLaws had never adjudicated a case quite like this one. Also, she had never enjoyed a case quite as much. Case #215 came to her bench on a Monday morning in July. A customer of the Cream Puff Heaven Patisserie filed a claim against the establishment's owners.

The plaintiff, Mr. Charles E. Claire, was the first to take the stand. He claimed that the patisserie was guilty of false advertising and deception. As the judge learned, Mr. Claire had regularly purchased four dozen cream puffs every day for 60 days. The patisserie, Claire reported, advertises that they use real whipping cream in all its pastries. Mr. Claire produced copies of the newspaper ads wherein the pastry maker claims to use only fresh, whole cream with no artificial ingredients.

"But this is untrue!" bellowed Mr. Claire, waving the ads. "The cream is fake! Customers are paying for real cream and getting artificial mush!"

The defendant, Lulu C. Custer, maintained her innocence. She held up large, empty cream cartons as evidence.

Judge DeLaws, more interested in finding the truth (or shall we say, in **tasting** the truth) than listening to hours of competing testimony, dispatched the bailiff to the patisserie to buy a dozen cream puffs. When he returned, the judge ate all twelve. She reached her decision while her mouth was still full. The cream was indeed artificial, she ruled. Mr. Claire was awarded $5,184 to compensate for the cost of 2,880 cream puffs.

What is the theme of this story?

Circle evidence in the story to defend the theme you chose.

Write a summary of this story's plot.

Name

A LIST OF IFS

The message of Kipling's famous poem can apply to males and females alike.

As you read it, decide what overall message (theme) the poet conveys.

"IF —"
by Rudyard Kipling

If you can keep your head when all about you
Are losing theirs and blaming it on you;
If you can trust yourself when all men doubt you
But make allowance for their doubting too;
If you can wait and not be tired by waiting, (5)
Or, being lied about, don't deal in lies,
Or, being hated, don't give way to hating,
And yet don't look too good, nor talk too wise;
If you can dream—and not make dreams your master;
If you can think—and not make thoughts your aim; (10)
If you can meet with Triumph and Disaster
And treat those two impostors just the same;
If you can bear to hear the truth you've spoken
Twisted by knaves to make a trap of fools,
Or watch the things you gave your life to broken, (15)
And stoop and build 'em up with worn-out tools;
If you can make one heap of all your winnings
And risk it on one turn of pitch-and-toss,
And lose, and start again at your beginnings
And never breathe a word about your loss;   (20)
If you can force your heart and nerve and sinew
To serve your turn long after they are gone,
And so hold on when there is nothing in you
Except the Will which says to them: "Hold on."
If you can talk with crowds and keep your virtue, (25)
Or walk with kings—nor lose the common touch;
If neither foes nor loving friends can hurt you;
If all men count with you, but none too much;
If you can fill the unforgiving minute
With sixty seconds' worth of distance run — (30)
Yours is the Earth and everything that's in it,
And, which is more, you'll be a Man, my son.

Work cited:
Kipling, Rudyard. "If." *Rewards and Fairies.*
Toronto: The Macmillan Company of Canada,
Ltd, 1910. 175-6. Print.

Name

26

Copyright © 2014 World Book, Inc./
Incentive Publications, Chicago, IL

A LIST OF IFS, CONTINUED

Use this graphic organizer to analyze the theme of this poem. In the middle box, write the theme of the poem. In the next layer of boxes, write some of the character traits (in your own words) that the poem mentions to advance the theme. (Use your own words.) In the outside layer, copy a phrase from the poem that describes or mentions each trait.

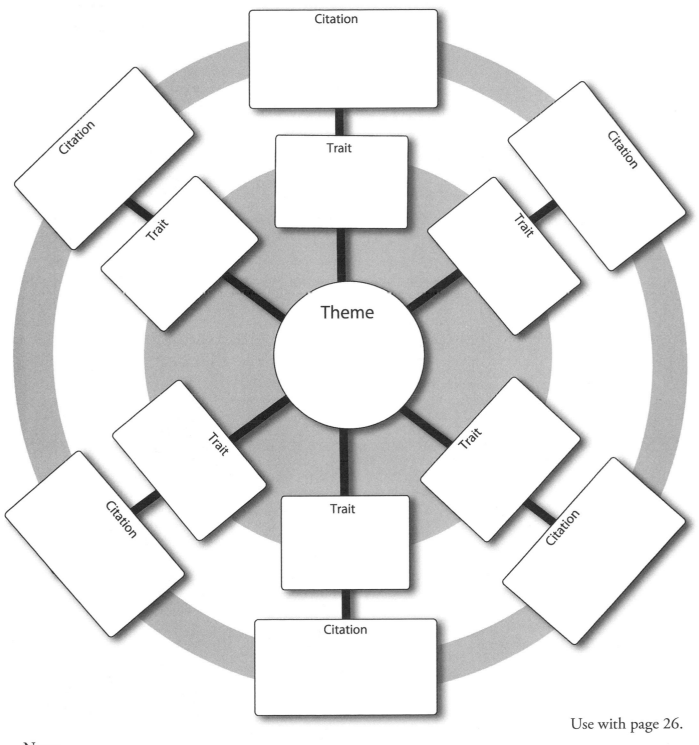

Use with page 26.

Name

Copyright © 2014 World Book, Inc./
Incentive Publications, Chicago, IL

Common Core Reinforcement Activities — 7th Grade Language

CAUGHT!

To summarize means to identify and re-tell the most important ideas in the text in a shorter, more concise way. When you summarize a passage, you will be able to understand it better and remember what you have read. A good summary includes a beginning, middle, and end; it also contains the main ideas along with some supporting details.

Read Agent Lee's Detective Log and summarize it on a separate piece of paper. Use your own words and be concise. Make sure you include a summary of the beginning, the actions of all suspects, and the conclusion.

Detective Log

January 8, 2014

Four suspects from our "Most Wanted" list have been apprehended. All are in the process of extradition to other states.

A clever sting operation brought the four smugglers to Washington's Dulles Airport within a four-hour period. Each suspect will face charges in the locations of the crimes they committed.

Lucinda Hertz, also known as ZaZa Hertzog, was apprehended while seeking veterinary help for an illegally imported, exotic Kagu bird.

Georgio Cabannara, also known as Gonzo Georges, tripped up when he sold a contraband potion (purported to cure baldness) to a federal agent wearing a fake bald scalp.

The third fugitive posed as a hip-hop artist while trafficking in pirated music and movies. **Martina Rioux** (using the performance name of Lady Sasha) accidentally fell from the stage during a concert stunt—literally into the arms of two double agents.

Aubrey DeBoer was perhaps the most ambitious of the smugglers and the last to be apprehended. Agents spotted him when a bird of paradise flew out of his suitcase. Closing in to search him and his luggage, they found two pygmy marmosets in his underwear, two Asian leopard cubs in another suitcase, and a steamer trunk full of elephant tusks. We've dubbed him "the guy who smuggled a whole zoo."

The successful operations left the nefarious four few alternatives but to submit to arrest. This is a great day for the agency.

Agent Suzannah Lee

Name

Copyright © 2014 World Book, Inc./
Incentive Publications, Chicago, IL

THE MISSING MASCOT

In this story, the main setting is a bank of five specific lockers in a school. Notice how the setting eventually reveals the details of the plot.

Mystery in the Locker Room

The mascot of the North Middle School Rams disappeared during the second half of the Saturday football game. Scouring the football field, stands, concession booths, and parking lot, frantic fans and school officials searched for Rambo, a small ram. Rambo was nowhere to be found. But on Monday morning, some clues began to turn up inside the school.

Five students, whose lockers were in a row (numbers 16, 17, 18, 19, and 20), could not get their lockers open. Even stranger, puzzling sounds, smells, and liquids emanated from the lockers. School administrators bustled about authoritatively, gruffly questioning students (in particular, the owners of the five lockers: Matt, Julio, Tiana, Andrew, and Meghan). The investigation revealed the following clues:

- One strange item was found in each of the five lockers.
- Locker number 19 contained a frightened, messy, squeaking rat.
- The ram was not in locker 17.
- Matt's locker was between Julio's and Andrew's.
- Tiana's locker had the lowest number.
- The locker next to Andrew's held a large garlic pizza.
- Locker 18 held no food.
- Officials found melting rootbeer snowballs in Meghan's locker.
- Andrew's locker is next to Tiana's.
- Another locker held a bag of spoiled Chinese food.

The clues were sufficient. A muzzled Rambo was found.

Follow the clues to solve the mystery and answer these questions. (It might help to draw a diagram.)

1. In which locker was Rambo found?

2. Who is the main suspect?

Name

ON SEEING AN ELEPHANT

The elements of a story (theme, setting, plot, characters, and conflict) add details to its meaning and development.

As you read this story, think about how its elements interact to make the story unique. Then answer the questions below.

The Blind Men and the Elephant

by John Godfrey Saxe

It was six men of Indostan
To learning much inclined,
Who went to see the Elephant
(Though all of them were blind),
That each by observation
Might satisfy his mind.

The **First** approached the Elephant,
And happening to fall
Against his broad and sturdy side,
At once began to bawl:
"God bless me! but the Elephant
Is very like a WALL!"

The **Second,** feeling of the tusk,
Cried, "Ho! What have we here
So very round and smooth and sharp?
To me 'tis mighty clear.
This wonder of an Elephant
Is very like a SPEAR!"

The **Third** approached the animal,
And happening to take
The squirming trunk within his hands,
Thus boldly up and spake:
"I see," quoth he, "the Elephant
Is very like a SNAKE!"

The **Fourth** reached out an eager hand,
And felt about the knee.
"What most this wondrous beast
Is like is mighty plain," quoth he;
" 'Tis clear enough the Elephant
Is very like a TREE!"

The **Fifth,** who chanced to touch the ear,
Said: "E'en the blindest man
Can tell what this resembles most;
Deny the fact who can.
This marvel of an Elephant
Is very like a FAN!"

The **Sixth** no sooner had begun
About the beast to grope,
Than, seizing on the swinging tail
That fell within his scope,
"I see," quoth he, "the Elephant
Is very like a ROPE!"

And so these men of Indostan
Disputed loud and long,
Each in his own opinion
Exceeding stiff and strong,
Though each was partly in the right,
And all were in the wrong!

Work cited:
Saxe, John Godfrey. "The Blind Men and the Elephant." *The Poetical Works of John Godfrey Saxe*. Boston: Houghton, Mifflin and Company, 1869. 135.

1. What is the setting of this story?

2. Who are the main characters?

3. What are the important points of the plot?

Name

Use with page 31.

Copyright © 2014 World Book, Inc./ Incentive Publications, Chicago, IL

ON SEEING AN ELEPHANT, CONTINUED

Answer these questions about how the elements of this story relate to each other.

4. What is the main conflict in this story?

5. How does the blindness of the men affect the plot development?

6. Could this story have a similar plot with a different setting? Explain why or why not.

Now fill out this diagram about the theme of the story. In the center, write what you think the theme is. In each circle, briefly describe how the characters (including the elephant) help to develop this theme.

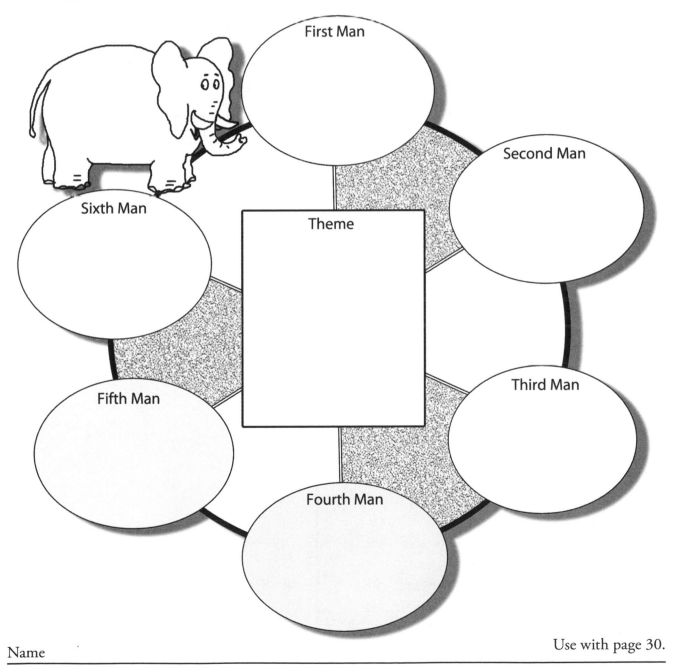

First Man

Second Man

Sixth Man

Theme

Third Man

Fifth Man

Fourth Man

Name

Use with page 30.

Copyright © 2014 World Book, Inc./
Incentive Publications, Chicago, IL

Common Core Reinforcement Activities — 7th Grade Language

SPIDER WATCHING

Love them or hate them, there is something mesmerizing about spiders! Maybe you've had some spider-watching experiences similar to these stories.

In many cases, you can figure out the meaning of a word by using clues in the words and sentences around it. As you read these passages, use the context of the bold words to help decide their meanings. Check your guesses with a dictionary.

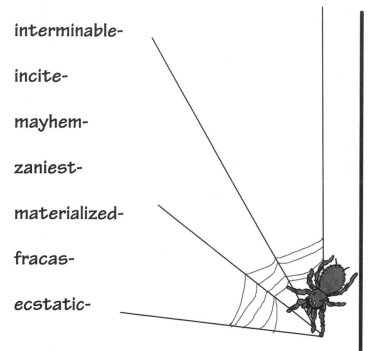

interminable-

incite-

mayhem-

zaniest-

materialized-

fracas-

ecstatic-

Reporters swarmed a suburban home today to get a picture of the **peculiar** spider. Not only is the itsy, bitsy spider (with only seven legs) an **anomaly**. Its behavior is **quirky** as well. This spider has been climbing a waterspout every day for two months. When rain **surges** through the waterspout, the spider vanishes. When the sun comes out, the spider begins its ascent up the waterspout. The owners of the home, fearing that eventually the spider will be washed away forever, have tried **myriad** plans to capture or relocate the spider; all have been **ineffectual**.

Mischievous Millie had an **interminable** habit of using her pet tarantula, Tom, to **incite mayhem**. The tarantula showed up in the **zaniest** situations—strutting along a Thanksgiving dinner table, slinking across an empty pew during a church service, or hanging from the teacher's desk during a math test. Once, a whole restaurant full of people emptied in seconds when Tom **materialized** between the pages of a menu. Tom terrified or delighted children and adults on numerous occasions. The shrieks and squeals never failed to cause a **fracas** wherever he went. This always left Millie **ecstatic**—beaming from ear to ear.

peculiar-

anomaly-

quirky-

surges-

myriad-

ineffectual-

Name

32

Copyright © 2014 World Book, Inc./
Incentive Publications, Chicago, IL

A ONE-SIDED CONVERSATION

Sometimes it takes more than one sentence to give you enough clues to solve the mystery of a word's meaning. This talkative young lady supplies plenty of clues!

Read Bianca's side of the conversation. Use the context to decide the meaning of each bold word. Share your definitions and discuss the reasons for your decisions.

I love to go to parties.
They set a happy mood.
The games and dancing draw me,
Though I mostly go for food.
This party has great music.
But the snacks—I don't see a bite!
The **paucity** of food disturbs me.
I'll be hungry the rest of the night.

I will never tell!
They can threaten
to torture me with
scorpions, but I will
never **divulge** your
secret.

You're rude.
You insult with intent.
I'd say you are
impertinent!

Chester hates
water. He hates sand.
Therefore, his friends
were **confounded** when
he showed up for the
beach party.

All the rest of us are
covered with itchy mosquito
bite lumps from the camping
trip. Charlie has no bumps or
itching, though I saw the
insects bite him. He must be
immune to mosquito bites.

I heard there
was a **dearth** of
tickets available.
That's why I went
down to the arena at
dawn to get in line
for the opening of
ticket sales at
noon today.

Angie has shown
that she is an **eclectic**
musician. Her show
combines rock music with
country music, classical
music, jazz, blues,
and hip-hop.

Name _____

Copyright © 2014 World Book, Inc./
Incentive Publications, Chicago, IL

Common Core Reinforcement Activities — 7th Grade Language

UNBELIEVABLE HEADLINES

Though it may be hard to believe, these headlines are related to events that really happened!

Use the context of the headline to make a guess about what each bold, italicized word means. Write your definitions below each headline.

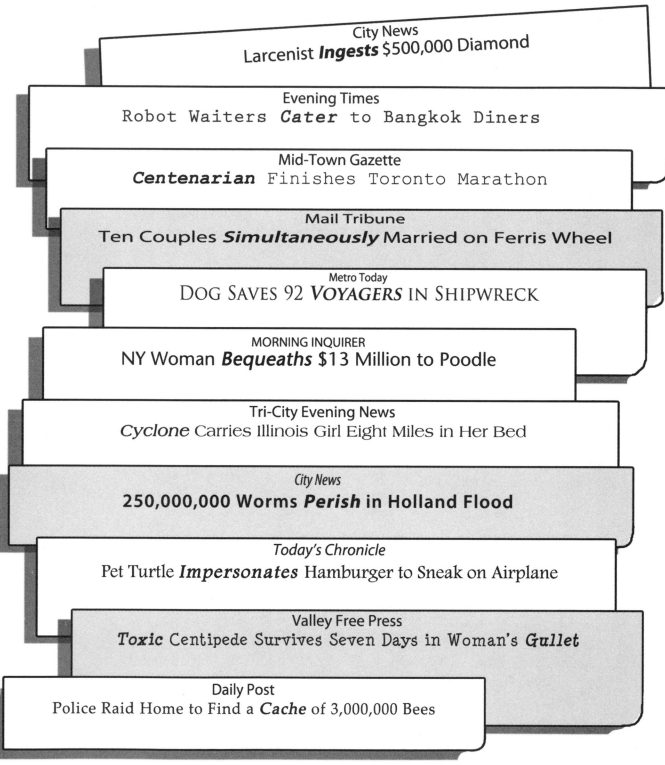

City News
Larcenist **_Ingests_** $500,000 Diamond

Evening Times
Robot Waiters **_Cater_** to Bangkok Diners

Mid-Town Gazette
Centenarian Finishes Toronto Marathon

Mail Tribune
Ten Couples **_Simultaneously_** Married on Ferris Wheel

Metro Today
DOG SAVES 92 **_VOYAGERS_** IN SHIPWRECK

MORNING INQUIRER
NY Woman **_Bequeaths_** $13 Million to Poodle

Tri-City Evening News
Cyclone Carries Illinois Girl Eight Miles in Her Bed

City News
250,000,000 Worms **_Perish_** in Holland Flood

Today's Chronicle
Pet Turtle **_Impersonates_** Hamburger to Sneak on Airplane

Valley Free Press
Toxic Centipede Survives Seven Days in Woman's **_Gullet_**

Daily Post
Police Raid Home to Find a **_Cache_** of 3,000,000 Bees

Name

34

Copyright © 2014 World Book, Inc./
Incentive Publications, Chicago, IL

PROMISES KEPT (OR NOT)

Often, poets use literary devices to add to the impact of a poem. These devices include rhyme (matching sounds at the end of lines), alliteration (repeating sounds at the beginning of words), and repetition (repeating entire words or phrases).

The Robert Frost poem "Stopping by Woods on a Snowy Evening" ends with a memorable statement about keeping promises. Find a copy of the Frost poem. Your school or public librarian can help. Read it and the poem below aloud. Then answer the questions. Finally, finish the statement in the speech balloon.

Promises
by Luke, Grade 8

Making a promise is like kissing a girl—
On the spur of a moment, it's easy to do.

When you wish you'd taken another course
You realize your options are only two:
Keep the promise and keep the girl
Or live with the anger directed at you.

Take my advice: think twice or thrice—
Keep your kisses and promises few.

Two promises that should always be kept are . . .

1.

2.

"But I have promises to keep"
Robert Lee Frost

1. What is the pattern of the rhyme in each poem?

2. How do these patterns affect the reader?

3. Circle one example of alliteration in each poem.

4. Where do the poets use repetition?

5. What is the impact of this repetition?

Name

GREEN IS . . .

Poets use many different structures to convey their ideas. A structure includes organization; line length; patterns in words, lines, rhythms, or rhymes; and visual layout. You can spot the structure with your eyes, but you can also hear it with your ears. Read a poem out loud whenever you can.

Answer these questions about the poem's structure. This will help you examine the poem closely to understand what the poet is trying to convey.

Green is the way a pickle pinches your
tongue, And the smell of a fluoride
treatment.

It's the rhythmic chirping of crickets
Or the croon of a slow country song.

Green oozes and goozes,
Sour and smooth.

Green is mold and jealousy,
Disappointment, and old cottage cheese.

You are green when your heart is broken
Or when you freeze up during a math test.

Green glazes your fingers with grease,
And tangles your tongue with grimy gristle.

It sprawls velvet over a golf course,
And lights up a neon bike shirt.

Green drips slime on a mischievous frog,
And lends the gurgle to a rushing stream.

A dazzling new idea is green—
Like the streaky teal tail of a comet.

You can trust green to be truthful.
You can take green to the bank!

Seventh Grade Class Collaboration

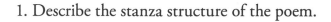

1. Describe the stanza structure of the poem.

2. What different organizational patterns do you find?

3. What effect might the poets want to create with this organization?

4. If this poem were one long stanza, would its effect or meaning be different? Explain your choice.

5. What literary devices can you find in this poem (such as alliteration, metaphor, simile, personification, rhyme, repetition, hyperbole, onomatopoeia)? Give two examples.

Name

Copyright © 2014 World Book, Inc./
Incentive Publications, Chicago, IL

SO MANY LAYERS

Poets use many different structures to convey their ideas. A structure includes organization; line length; patterns in words, lines, rhythms, or rhymes; and visual layout.

Answer these questions about the poem's structure. This will help you examine the poem closely to understand what the poet is trying to convey.

1. Describe the structure of this poem.

2. What is the message of this poem?

3. Why does the poet arrange the lines in this unique way?

4. How does the poet compare herself to an onion?

5. Circle words or phrases that are repetitive. What effect does the repetition have on the tone or message of the poem?

I Am an Onion
by Samantha , Grade 7

I am an onion
     covered with layers of layers,
each one fragile.
     Yet with so many,
their papery strength protects me.

If you dare,
     peel my layers away—
       careful now.
As you lift each one,
     as it crumbles,
       you get closer
to my true taste and scent—
     closer to who I really am.

Like the onion
     whose strong smell
pushes some tasters away,
       I have a scent that says,
"Beware. Leave me alone."

If you will go to the trouble
     to keep peeling, peeling,
if you are not afraid
     of the tears that grow
       as layers are exposed,
you'll find that my distinct taste
     like the onion's,
       will add flavor to your life.

Name

Copyright © 2014 World Book, Inc./
Incentive Publications, Chicago, IL

Common Core Reinforcement Activities — 7th Grade Language

CONFLICTING VERSIONS

Different characters in an event experience or see the event differently. This article contains several points of view of the same incident.

Read the article and discuss the points of view with a partner. Whose point of view do you believe? Give evidence from the text to support your answer.

| Volume 139 | **WOODLAND TIMES** | Tuesday, August 19 |

Woodcutter Praised for Daring Rescue

(Red Bluffs, California) Quick thinking and bold action saved the life of a local girl yesterday. Woody Axle, a northern California timber worker, was awarded a medal of honor today for rescuing Ms. Red R. Hood from the jaws of a hungry wolf.

Mr. Axle reported that he was cutting trees east of town when he heard cries. He said that he followed the sounds to a small house at 286 Green Trail Lane, found a girl inside the house trapped by a wolf, and overpowered the wolf with his axe. Axle called 911 immediately.

According to Mrs. Agatha R. Hood, grandmother of the girl and owner of the home, she was alone when the wolf forcibly entered the dwelling around midday Monday. The wolf allegedly snatched her bonnet and gown, tied her up, and locked her in the closet. When Mr. Axle arrived at the scene, the wolf was wearing the grandmother's nightgown and nightcap. Apparently the wolf donned grandma's clothing, climbed in her bed, and awaited the arrival of the granddaughter.

Woody Axle caught this picture of the wolf in Mrs. Hood's night clothing.

Mrs. Hood, through her attorney, gave a statement that the wolf locked her in her closet after taking her bonnet and robe.

Young Ms. Hood was treated for a broken arm and abrasions at nearby Storyland Hospital. Mrs. Hood was unharmed.

The Department of Fish and Wildlife and the California Humane Society have issued complaints against Mr. Axle, claiming cruel treatment of the wolf—a member of an endangered species.

Name

Copyright © 2014 World Book, Inc./ Incentive Publications, Chicago, IL

HEARING VOICES

Just as different people can have different points of view about a similar event, different characters in a story can have their own points of view.

As you read this story, think about each character and the point of view he or she expresses. Then answer the questions. Circle parts of the text that support your answers.

Trust the camel!

"Voices will speak to you in the desert. When they do—listen to them." Before they left on their expedition, the twins heard this advice from a foolish old woman who filled them with desert superstitions and tales of dubious credibility. They had given little thought to the woman's words.

A raging sandstorm had surrounded the group quickly. Fierce winds, stinging sand, and blackening skies sent them to huddle beside the camels. By the time the sand cleared, it was dark. Todd and Tara dug themselves out and found they were alone. Their guide and the other travelers were nowhere in sight. All they could see in every direction was empty sand. They had no food, little water, and no idea what to do.

For what seemed like hours, they huddled together in fear, consoled only by the steady breathing of the sleeping camel. Abruptly, a crooked little spiral of sand scuttled past, whistling and whispering: "Trust the camel." At least that is what Todd thought he heard. Tara heard nothing.

Again, the whirlwind circled. Again, a voice whispered, "Trust the camel." Again, Tara heard nothing.

Strange as the voice in the wind seemed, its message made sense to Todd. In his desperation, he grasped at this feeble bit of hope. The twins had always been told that, if lost, they should stay in one place. Perhaps it was the words of the old woman that nudged them away from heeding that advice. Tara scrambled up onto the camel and prodded him awake. Slowly, the sluggish camel struggled to its feet. Trudging through the sand, following some inner compass, he moved toward a destination that Todd and Tara did not understand. Todd just kept remembering the whisper: "Trust the camel." Tara did her best to trust Todd—and the camel.

When, after several fretful hours, the shapes of other camels and people appeared on the horizon, the twins breathed a deep, combined sigh of relief. Their risky choice had led to rescue—not disaster.

1. How do Todd's and Tara's viewpoints differ?

2. What is the narrator's point of view?

3. Whose point of view changes? How can you tell?

Name

HISTORY RE-IMAGINED

Historical fiction is a genre of literature in which a writer re-imagines important events in history. In Henry Wadsworth Longfellow's famous poem "Paul Revere's Ride," he tells the tale of one man's role in the American Revolution. But how much of the poem is factual? How much is imagined?

Locate and read a copy of the original poem. Your school or public librarian can help. Then read the factual account below. Finally, use the diagram on the following page to compare and contrast the two selections.

Paul Revere was an American craftsman and patriot who made numerous contributions to the American Revolution, including his famous ride to warn his fellow patriots of an impending British attack.

In 1775, King George III instructed his British commanders in America to restore order to the colonies. He sent 700 men to Concord, Massachusetts, to destroy the colonists' supplies and arrest the disloyal patriots, including Samuel Adams and John Hancock.

The British troops assembled on the evening of April 18th. The patriots had heard rumblings of this movement and were preparing to defend themselves. Patriot leader Joseph Warren sent Paul Revere and another patriot, William Dawes, to warn their own troops in Lexington and Concord. Revere arranged for a signal to be sent from the Old North Church in Boston: two lanterns meant the British were coming by water; one lantern meant they were arriving by land.

Revere borrowed a horse and left Boston around 10:00 p.m. He arrived in Lexington around midnight, and joined William Dawes and Samuel Prescott for the ride to Concord. Unfortunately, they were surprised by a British patrol on their way; Prescott and Dawes escaped, but Revere was captured. He was later released, but without his horse. He made his way to Concord, where he joined Adams and Hancock. The men fled to safety, and when the British troops arrived, the patriots were armed and waiting.

Work cited:
"Revere, Paul." *World Book Student*. World Book, 2013. Web. 14 Sept. 2013.
© World Book, Inc. All rights reserved. Used by permission.

Name

Use with page 41.

HISTORY RE-IMAGINED, CONTINUED

Use this diagram to compare and contrast the two versions of Paul Revere's historic ride. In the left circle, include things that are found only in the poem. In the right circle, include facts and events that are found only in the historical account. In the middle, put any ideas that are found in both accounts.

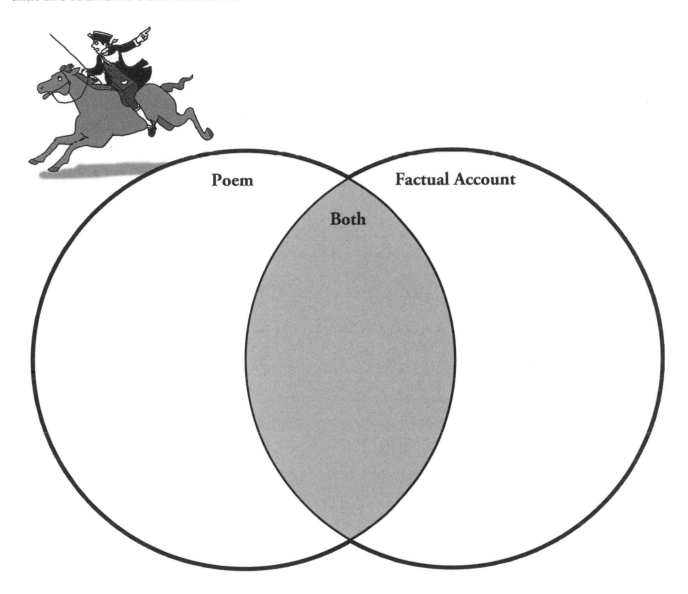

1. Why do you think the poet chose to re-imagine some of the historical facts?

2. How is the impact or effect of the two versions different?

Use with page 40.

Name

Copyright © 2014 World Book, Inc./
Incentive Publications, Chicago, IL

A DIFFERENT LOOK

Many works of literature (poems, plays, novels, etc.) have been remade into films or other visual presentations. Think about the movie versions of books you have read.

Choose a story that you can find in a text version and a visual version. Your school or public librarian can help. Make sure you have read and viewed the story recently. Use this form to compare and contrast two different versions.

	Written Version	Film Version
Title of the work		
Major characters		
Setting(s)		
Theme(s) or message(s)		

1. What, if any, major differences did you notice in the storylines of the two versions?

2. What visual and/or audio techniques did the filmmaker use to enhance the story?

3. How did the medium affect the impact of the story?

4. If a friend could experience only one version of the story, which one would you tell him or her to choose? Explain your reasons.

Name

READING

INFORMATIONAL TEXT

Grade 7

THE LOST EMPIRE

Understanding nonfiction requires many of the same skills needed to read fiction. Strategies such as paraphrasing, summarizing, asking questions, and picturing the images in your mind will help you understand and remember what you read. You should also be able to point to evidence in the text to confirm your ideas.

Read this article about Atlantis and answer the questions.

For centuries, people have been fascinated with Plato's tales about the legendary continent of Atlantis and its cataclysmic destruction. Ancient Greek philosopher Plato wove a tale of a great empire centered on an island continent created by Poseidon, god of the sea. Half-human and half-god creatures built great cities, and Atlantis became a great naval power.

According to the story, the people of Atlantis became arrogant and greedy after many prosperous years. They ignored Poseidon's laws that had kept the civilization running smoothly. The gods punished Atlantis with fire and earthquakes, bringing on floods and storms that destroyed the civilization.

For centuries, this story has ignited the imagination of listeners and readers as philosophers and scientists have debated the existence of Atlantis. Many describe the story as another Greek myth. Yet Plato is known to have mixed fable and fact in his writings. Some think the great city still lies beneath the ocean, inhabited by sea creatures such as mermaids and mermen. Expeditions have sought, unsuccessfully, to discover the remains of the civilization.

The group of three islands known as Santorini (now Thira) in the Aegean Sea was mostly destroyed by a volcanic eruption in 1625 B.C. Much of the land disappeared beneath the sea. A nearby civilization, the Minoans, inexplicably disappeared at about the same time. Some scholars surmise that these verified events influenced Plato's account. Recently, German physicist Rainer Kuhne and Swiss geographer Ulf Erlingsson have each argued that geographical data reveals islands (one near Spain, one in Ireland) that match Plato's description of Atlantis. Perhaps Plato had evidence of something that really happened beneath the sea—something that today's scientists cannot explain.

1. What evidence in the article points to the conclusion that Atlantis was a product of Plato's imagination? Use a red pen or pencil to circle this evidence.

2. What evidence in the article points to the conclusion that Atlantis was a real place? Use a blue pen or pencil to circle this evidence.

Works consulted:
Lovgren, Stefan. "Atlantis 'Evidence' Found in Spain and Ireland."
National Geographic News. National Geographic Society, 19 Aug. 2004. Web. 15 Sept. 2013.
Littleton, C. Scott. "Atlantis." *World Book Student*. World Book, 2013. Web. 17 Oct. 2013.

Name

SPELUNKING SAFELY

Sometimes information is given explicitly (stated outright). But often, you can figure out other details by discovering what the text infers (hints at) but does not state directly. The guidelines for safe spelunking (exploring underground caves) give explicit rules but leave lots of room for inferences about caves and spelunking.

Draw some inferences (logical conclusions based on evidence) about information that is not explicitly stated. On each line below, write something you can infer from the guidelines. Next to the bullet points, quote the evidence from the text that supports your conclusions. The first one is started for you.

1. Caves are very dark.

• "Take at least three long-lasting light sources."

•

•

2. _____

•

•

•

3. _____

•

•

•

4. _____

•

•

•

SAFE-CAVING GUIDELINES

1. Never cave alone. Plan to go with three or more people.

2. Let someone outside the cave know where and when you are going and when you will return.

3. Check the weather before you go into the cave. Make sure there is no danger of the cave flooding. (Avoid rainy days.)

4. Wear substantial clothing in layers. Your outer layer should be waterproof. If you are going into caves with water, wear a wetsuit.

5. Wear sturdy shoes or boots.

6. Eat and drink plenty of food and water.

7. Take at least three long-lasting light sources.

8. Wear a helmet at all times while in the cave.

9. Don't touch bats or other cave dwellers.

10. Always keep the person behind you in sight.

11. Know the way out of the cave. As you go along, mark the return route.

12. Take more time for your exit than your entrance. Depending on the structure of the cave, you may be climbing upwards to exit, and this can be harder than climbing down. Also, you will be tired at the end of your caving trip (and possibly cold and wet, too).

Name _____

Copyright © 2014 World Book, Inc./
Incentive Publications, Chicago, IL

Common Core Reinforcement Activities — 7th Grade Language

ONE GOOEY MESS

A molasses massacre—what on Earth could this be about? To explain this strange headline, use your sharpest reading skills to search for the central ideas.

As you read this article, look for three main ideas and pay attention to the way they are developed.

Molasses Massacre in Honolulu Harbor

September 13, 2013

A pipeline running from storage tanks to ships in Honolulu Harbor in Hawaii ruptured on September 9, spilling up to 233,000 gallons (882 million cubic meters) of molasses into the bay. Divers report that the spill has turned Honolulu Harbor into an environmental disaster area, with thousands upon thousands of fish and other marine creatures dead from suffocation. "Because the molasses is heavier than water, it is settling to the ocean floor, displacing oxygen-rich water that marine life need to breathe," said Keith Korsmeyer, professor of biology at Hawaii Pacific University.

The shipping company that owns the pipeline, Matson Navigation, has issued a statement regretting the spill but contending that there is nothing it can do to clean up the mess. Molasses is a sugar product that, unlike oil, will dissolve over time. However, scientists expect that the dissolved sugar will encourage the growth of bacteria, resulting in blooms (dense populations) that will also sap oxygen from the water. "This is the worst environmental damage to sea life that I have come across, and it's fair to say this is a biggie, if not the biggest that we've had to confront in the state of Hawaii," Gary Gill, deputy director for the Environmental Health Division of the U.S. Health Department, stated in an interview with Honolulu's NBC affiliate, KHNL.

Marine biologists worry that the fish die-off will lure such predators as sharks, barracuda, and eels into the harbor and into neighboring Keehi Lagoon, a major recreational area. Health officials in Hawaii warned swimmers, snorkelers, and surfers to stay out of the waters near the harbor. Molasses is manufactured at Hawaii's last sugar cane plantation and is transported by ship to the mainland.

Work cited:
"Behind the Headlines: Molasses Massacre in Honolulu Harbor."
World Book Student. World Book, 13 Sept. 2013. Web. 13 Sept. 2013.
© World Book, Inc. All rights reserved. Used by permission.

Write three main ideas from this article. Then complete the organizer on the next page (page 47).

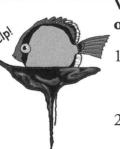

1.

2.

3.

Name _____

Use with page 47.

ONE GOOEY MESS, CONTINUED

Use this organizer to help you analyze the article from page 46. In each of the three top boxes, write one of the main ideas. In the two smaller boxes, write evidence from the article that supports each of the main ideas. At the bottom, write a summary (no longer than two sentences) of the passage.

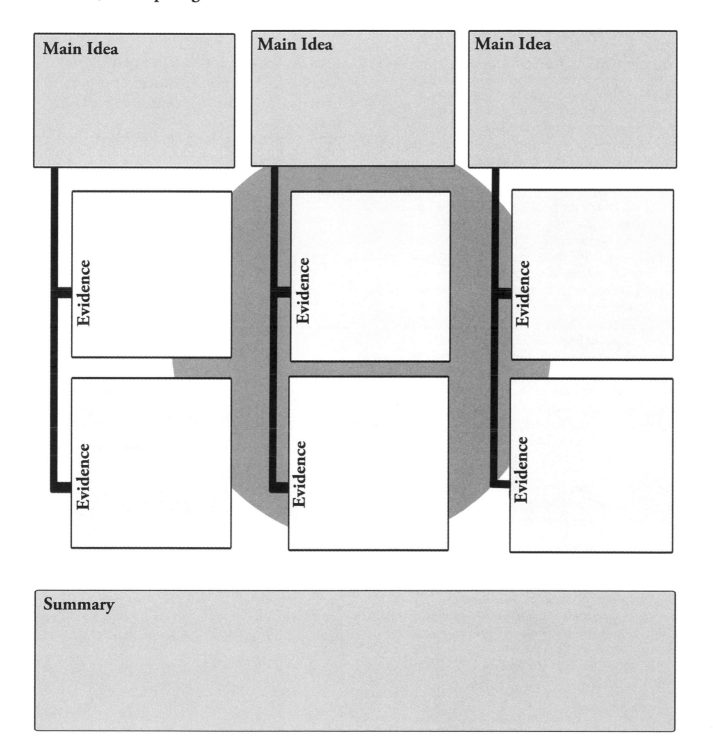

Main Idea

Main Idea

Main Idea

Evidence

Evidence

Evidence

Evidence

Evidence

Evidence

Summary

Use with page 46.

Name

Copyright © 2014 World Book, Inc./
Incentive Publications, Chicago, IL

Common Core Reinforcement Activities — 7th Grade Language

THE TALKING PENCIL

I'm complicated!

A **review** is a familiar form of nonfiction writing. In a review, an author gives his or her opinion about such things as a movie, book, article, performance, or restaurant. The opinion is supported by evidence. As you read this review of "I, Pencil," look for the writer's central idea and the evidence he uses to support it.

Review of "I, Pencil" Reviewer, Lucas Vega

"I, Pencil" is a fascinating essay by Leonard E. Read. It became popular when retold by Milton Friedman, 1976 Nobel Prize winner in economics. (You can even hear the story on YouTube.) Friedman begins his presentation with "Look at this pencil. There's not a single person in the world who could make this pencil."

The story, as told by the pencil, explains that the process of making a pencil actually takes hundreds of little steps that no single person can do. It takes many people to manufacture, sell, and deliver this product. Someone makes the chainsaw and other equipment used to cut wood. Others go into the forest to do the logging. Still others buy, transport, and mill the wood. In another part of the world, usually South America, the material for the pencil lead (graphite) is mined from the ground. Someone makes, sells, and delivers the mining equipment. Others dig the graphite. Still others buy, sell, and ship it to the pencil companies. The substance for the eraser comes from yet another part of the world. Someone taps rubber trees in Malaysia. This milky-white fluid goes through many stages of preparation, buying, selling, shipping, and delivering before it reaches the pencil manufacturer.

By the time all the supplies reach the place where the pencils are made, hundreds, perhaps thousands, of people from all over the world have participated.

The making of a pencil is a poignant example of how people who do not even know each other work together to produce a product. The purpose of the story, however, goes far beyond this lesson. Leonard Read told this to remark on the wonders of the free market economy and to show the price system in operation. Even with thousands of workers involved, the free market works to keep the product affordable. His memorable parable cleverly teaches a lesson in economics.

Work consulted:
Read, Leonard E. "I, Pencil." *Essays on Liberty, Volume VI.* Irvington, NY: The Foundation for Economic Education, Inc., 1959. 371-79.

Work cited:
Friedman, Milton. "I, Pencil." *YouTube.* 20 July 2012. Web. 3 Sept. 2013.

Name

Identify what you think are two central ideas in this review. Identify some pieces of evidence in the text that support each main idea.

Main Idea:

Evidence:

Main Idea:

Evidence:

Copyright © 2014 World Book, Inc./ Incentive Publications, Chicago, IL

RECORD-SETTING SUMMARIES

To *summarize* means to identify and re-tell the most important ideas in the text in a shorter, more concise way. Being able to summarize, both during and after reading, will help you remember information more easily.

Read each of the five passages below. Beneath each passage, write a concise one-sentence summary of what you read.

A. **Which Is Easier?**

Walking on water is a difficult feat. Yet, it seems that walking on your hands may be even harder. Just take a look at what the world records show. A water-walker covered 3,502 miles (5,636 km) on skis to set the world record. The record-holder who walked on his hands, however, covered only 870 miles (1,400 km).

B. Instead of celebrating Valentine's Day with flowers or a card, why not show your love by setting a Guinness World Record? On February 14, 2001, 34 couples from 22 countries simultaneously exchanged wedding vows 11 yards (10 m) underwater near Kradan Island, off the coast of Thailand, to set the record for most couples married underwater simultaneously. In 2007, 6,980 couples kissed in Tuzla, Bosnia, to set a record for most couples kissing simultaneously. Next year, express your love by setting a one-of-a-kind record.

C. Some people set records for active feats
Of speed or strength or skill.
But did you know that prizes go
To folks who just are still?
Some dive from planes or walk on ropes.
Some juggle two-edged swords.
To win renown, some wrestle snakes
Or surf through the air on boards.
But records can be broken
For doing nothing at all.
For standing still, sitting in trees,
Or relaxing on a wall.

D. The three little pigs had fun with the phrase, "Not by the hair on my chinny, chin, chin." I wonder if they ever considered trying for any of the Guinness World Records involving chins—such as the longest beard (17.5 feet/5 m), or the most glasses balanced on a chin (50), or the most chin-ups performed (5,045).

E. **Could YOU be a record setter?**
If you want to hold a Guinness World Record, you will need to do something better than anyone else in the world. First, read all of the current records. Decide if you will try to break an existing record or set a new one. Write to Guinness Records to get the guidelines. Keep careful notes on your record attempts. Two reliable persons or organizations must act as witnesses. Each record attempt must be recorded on videotape. Can you do it? Give it a try!

Works consulted: *Guinness World Records 2013*. New York: Bantam Books, 2013. Print.
Guinness World Records 2014. London: Guinness World Records Limited, 2013. Print.

Name

Copyright © 2014 World Book, Inc./
Incentive Publications, Chicago, IL

Common Core Reinforcement Activities — 7th Grade Language

CLIMBING FEVER

Interview with an ACW Climber

Interviewer: What in the world is an ACW, anyway?

Climber: It's the key feature in a great new sport. ACW is an artificial climbing wall.

Interviewer: Describe these walls.

Climber: The walls are not the rocks climbed in natural outdoor settings. They are artificially constructed walls, created with materials other than rock, mostly intended for indoor climbing. Various materials are used for the walls—wood, brick, or thick multiplex board. The walls have holes and grips for hands and feet. Some may have places to attach climbing ropes.

Interviewer: To me, one of the joys of climbing is to be outdoors. Why would I want to climb an ACW instead of a real rock?

Climber: There are so many reasons. You can get to the walls without long hikes. You don't have to worry about weather conditions or special clothing. You can practice climbing skills in a safe setting that is not extremely high. You can climb day or night. You can compete with and learn from many other climbers.

Interviewer: Is an ACW more appealing than real rocks to most climbers?

Climber: Everybody is happier climbing an ACW because it is safer.

Interviewer: Why do you think this is such a fast-growing sport?

Climber: ACW is safe and accessible to beginners. Because of that, many more people are learning to climb. It is so much fun. Everyone should do this!

Interviewer: Thank you for your time. I just might try this!

One of the most interesting aspects of an interview—whether you watch it, read it, listen to it, or participate in it—is the interaction between the interviewer and the person(s) being interviewed.

As you read this text, pay attention to the interaction between the ACW climber and the interviewer. Then answer the questions.

1. How does the interviewer seem to feel about the climber's ideas at the beginning of the interview? Give evidence from the text to support your answer.

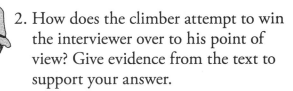

2. How does the climber attempt to win the interviewer over to his point of view? Give evidence from the text to support your answer.

3. In the end, does the interviewer's opinion seem to change? Give evidence from the text to support your answer.

Name

Copyright © 2014 World Book, Inc./ Incentive Publications, Chicago, IL

GUMBALL DILEMMA

Many nonfiction passages contain information that help the reader (or a character in the passage) learn something new or solidify some understanding. Even gumballs have something to teach you!

Read the essay, and analyze Charlie's interactions with the events.

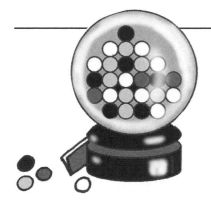

Probably Red or Probably Not?

Chelsea, grade 7

"I really want a red gumball. I wonder what the chances are that I will get one," Charlie thinks to himself as he stands in front of the gumball machine with his coin. He's not sure about using his last remaining coin, because there are so many nonred gumballs in the machine. The storeowner tells Charlie that she just filled the machine and she knows it has 60 red gumballs, 160 yellow gumballs, and 20 blue gumballs. Now Charlie can get an answer to his question—if only he can remember his math lessons on probability.

Probability is the chance or likelihood that something will happen. The result of an action, such as getting a gumball out of this machine, is called an ***outcome***. An ***event*** is a **particular** outcome. Charlie wants this event to be getting a red gumball. A number from zero through one is used to describe the probability of some event happening. If the bubblegum machine contains no red gumballs, then the chance of a red outcome is zero. If the machine contains all red gumballs, the probability of a red outcome is one. Since this machine does have some red ones, the probability of him getting red will be a fractional number between zero and one.

First of all, Charlie must find the total number of possible outcomes. This takes simple addition. He adds 60, 160, and 20 to find the sum of 240. There are 240 different gumballs that could come out. Next, Charlie needs to remember how to find probability of a single event: **The probability of an event is equal to the number of possible events divided by the total number of possible outcomes.** The number of possible outcomes in this case is 240. The number of red events possible is 60. The probability of getting a red gumball for Charlie, then, is 60 divided by 240, or one-fourth. He has one chance in four of getting a red gumball. He decides that these are good odds—worth spending his last coin.

Charlie puts his coin in and gets a yellow gumball. Now, he wonders what his chances will be of getting red if he were to try again. He realizes that the number in the gumball machine has changed, so it's a new problem. But he doesn't have another coin, so we won't be solving that one today!

1. What does Charlie remember about the specific probability of getting what he wants?

2. How does Charlie's decision-making process change throughout the story?

Name

Copyright © 2014 World Book, Inc./
Incentive Publications, Chicago, IL

Common Core Reinforcement Activities — 7th Grade Language

STEPHANIE'S COOL INVENTION

complex polymer structure

Nonfiction frequently contains technical or unfamiliar vocabulary. Sometimes the context of a sentence or paragraph gives clues to a word's meaning. However, it might be necessary to consult a dictionary or other reference source.

Read this biography and use the context of each bold word to predict its meaning. Write your predictions below. Then check your guesses in a dictionary. Remember, you are looking for the meaning that fits this specific text.

Kwolek, Stephanie Louise (1923-...), an American researcher, is the inventor of Kevlar, a **fiber** five times as strong as steel. Kwolek did much of her research at the DuPont Company, a chemical company where she worked for 40 years. She retired in 1986, holding 17 single or joint patents. Kwolek later worked as a **consultant** to DuPont and to the National Academy of Sciences, which advises the U.S. government on scientific matters. In 1996, she received the National Medal of Technology, the highest prize for technological **innovation** in the United States.

Kwolek was born on July 31, 1923, in New Kensington, Pennsylvania. In 1946, she earned a Bachelor of Science degree from Margaret Morrison college, the women's branch of the Carnegie Institute of Technology (now Carnegie-Mellon University). That year, Kwolek joined DuPont. Her team worked to create and test new *polymers*, long chain molecules created by linking smaller molecules. Polymers can be spun into fibers and made into fabric or plastics.

In 1964, DuPont asked Kwolek to find a strong, lightweight fiber to replace steel in **reinforcing** car tires. In 1965, Kwolek found such a polymer, eventually called Kevlar. The polymer's molecules form liquid crystals when dissolved. When spun into solid fibers, the molecules line up facing the same direction. This structure gives the material **extraordinary** strength and stiffness.

By 1971, DuPont started **commercial** manufacture of Kevlar. Police officers began using Kevlar body armor in 1975. Protective vests made from multiple layers of Kevlar are lightweight but can stop many types of bullets. Kevlar has saved thousands of law enforcement officers from death or disabling injury. The U.S. military also adopted Kevlar body armor, helmets, and vehicle liners to reduce **casualties** in wars. Kevlar is also used in brake pads, motorcycle helmets, bridge cables, skis, airplane and spacecraft parts, belted tires, and other items.

Work cited:
Bix, Amy Sue. "Kwolek, Stephanie Louise." *World Book Student*. World Book, 2013. Web. 14 Sept. 2013.
© World Book, Inc. All rights reserved. Used by permission.

fiber-

consultant-

innovation-

reinforcing-

extraordinary-

commercial-

casualties-

Name

Copyright © 2014 World Book, Inc./ Incentive Publications, Chicago, IL

TO MAKE A MUMMY

You have probably seen pictures of mummies (real ones or maybe costumes). You may have even pretended to be one! But did you know that it took the ancient Egyptians up to 70 days to complete the steps necessary to mummify a dead body?

Read the steps below and discuss the meaning of each bold vocabulary word with a partner. Work together to think of a synonym or short definition for each word. Finally, re-read the steps to other classmates—substituting your synonyms or definitions as you read.

The Making of a Mummy

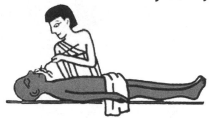

Step 1: The body was washed with water from the Nile River mixed with palm wine. Body organs were extracted through a slit in the side. The brain was removed through the nostrils or a small hole poked in the back of the head. Sometimes the heart was replaced with a stone **scarab amulet**.

Step 2: The organs were sealed in canopic jars. A carving representing the organ and the god who would protect the journey into the afterlife decorated the top of each jar. The jars were placed in a chest that went into the tomb with the mummy.

Step 3: The empty space inside the body was packed in *natron*, a substance that helped to **dehydrate** the body.

Step 4: After 40 days, the body was cleaned with fragrant oils and the **cavity** was filled with **aromatic** spices.

Step 5: The body was wrapped with many, many layers of linen strips.

Step 6: The body was **adorned** with **sacred** jewelry and a golden mask carved to look like the face of the dead person.

Step 7: The finished mummy was placed in a coffin within a coffin within a coffin. It was then lowered into a stone **sarcophagus** deep inside the tomb.

Work consulted:
"How Mummies Are Made." *PBS.org*. Public Broadcasting System. n.d. Web. 7 Sept. 2013.

Name _____

DISASTER AT SEA

This nonfiction piece summarizes the tragic story of the ship *Titanic*.

As you read, think about how the author paints a picture of the history of the event. Then follow the directions and answer the questions following the passage.

They called her "unsinkable" but the *Titanic* was not. They called her "a floating luxury hotel"—and indeed she was! The ship was a grand palace with huge rooms, gold-plated light fixtures, a swimming pool, and steam baths. No ship this colossal or opulent had ever been built before.

Hundreds of passengers boarded the *Titanic* in Southampton, England, on April 10, 1912. The great new ship was bound for New York on its maiden voyage. At a half hour past midnight on her fourth day at sea, disaster struck the *Titanic*. Actually, the *Titanic* struck disaster in the form of an iceberg. Despite several warnings of ice in the sea, the ship was traveling near her maximum speed when her starboard side struck the berg, tearing open five compartments. A command went out for people to get into the lifeboats. Regrettably, the company that built the ship had installed only enough lifeboats for half the people on board. In their arrogance, the owners were convinced that the ship was invincible.

The *Titanic* sent out distress signals hoping nearby vessels would come to help. After only three hours, in a perpendicular position, the ship sank with many of her lights still shining. Another ship, the *Carpathia*, arrived the next day to rescue 705 survivors. About 1,520 passengers and crew members perished.

The sinking of the *Titanic* was followed by fury over the shortage of lifeboats, the lack of a good evacuation plan, what seemed like the carelessness of the pilot, and the unequal treatment of passengers on board. Theories abound about why the *Titanic* sank. Seventy-five years later, the ship's wreckage was found. Small submarines have explored the wreckage, and many artifacts have been recovered. Perhaps some of the mysteries of this disaster will now be solved.

Work consulted:
"Titanic." *History.com.* A & E Television Networks, 2013. Web. 18 Sept. 2013.

1. Read the passage again, and highlight or underline specific words the author uses to paint a picture of the ship and the events.

2. What words or phrases suggest that the disaster could have been avoided?

3. What words or phrases give clues as to the writer's viewpoint of the event?

Name

GOT GRIT?

The specific words an author chooses can have a powerful impact on the reader.

As you read the advertising poster, pay attention to the impact of specific words chosen by the writer.

1. Who is the intended audience for this ad? How do you know?

2. Locate these adjectives in the ad: *speeding, undaunted, precarious, parlous, spine-chilling.*
   What is the tone set by these words?

3. What does "Feel the adrenaline rush!" mean as used here?

4. How does the last line, "PURSUE YOUR WILDEST DREAMS TODAY," contribute to the
   tone of the ad?

Name

AMAZING JOURNEYS

The structure of a text can add to its meaning and impact. Writers generally craft the structure of a text carefully to create a particular impact, set a mood, convey meaning, or for some other effect.

As you read this passage about record-setting journeys, consider why the writer may have chosen to structure the text in this way.

What people will do for a record-setting journey! I had no idea there were so many possibilities for trips. I expected people to attempt record distances on motorcycles, in fast cars, on bikes or skis, in trucks, in hot air balloons, or swimming across large bodies of water. But the most astounding journeys are completed on lawnmowers, soap box cars, skateboards, roller skates, stilts, taxis, school buses, unicycles, snowboards, snowmobiles, and golf carts. Some folks leave the ground to set records in the water or air—with jet skis, hang gliders, canoes, kayaks, or water skis. They travel in coffee-powered cars, wheelchairs, fire engines, and rickshaws. Some venture long distances paddling a bathtub, giving a friend a ride in a wheelbarrow, or pulling a train with their teeth. One adventuresome young man, Tony Hawks, set one record hitchhiking around the circumference of Ireland. This might not seem all that impressive, except that he hitchhiked the whole way with a refrigerator. Hurray for the human imagination!

Works consulted: *Guinness World Records 2013.* New York: Bantam Books, 2013. Print.
Guinness World Records 2014. London: Guinness World Records Limited, 2013. Print.

1. How is the information in this passage organized?

2. What are the main components of this passage?

3. How does this structure contribute to the author's purpose? Explain your answer.

Name

QUITE BY ACCIDENT

SILLY PUTTY®—Engineer James Wright was trying to invent a synthetic rubber. He mixed boric acid and silicon oil—and it turned into a fun, bouncy, stretchy-but-breakable substance that picked up pictures and print from newspaper pages.

POPSICLE®—Eleven-year old Frank Epperon left a drink mixture outside in a container that had a stirring stick in it. That night, temperatures dropped below freezing, and in the morning, he discovered the liquid frozen to the stick.

PLAY-DOH®—Soap manufacturer Noah McVicker set out to produce a wallpaper cleaner. His nephew found that he could use the substance as a non-messy modeling clay, and eventually started a company just to make the substance for play.

CHOCOLATE CHIP COOKIE—Inn owner Ruth Wakefield ran out of baker's chocolate when she was making "butter drop do" cookies. She broke up some pieces of semi-sweet chocolate, assuming the pieces would melt and make chocolate batter. But the chocolate stayed in pieces and a popular cookie was created!

MICROWAVE OVEN—Engineer Percy Spencer worked around microwave magnetrons (electron tubes for generating microwaves). One day when he paused in front of a magnetron, the candy bar in his pocket melted. That gave him the idea for using microwaves to for cooking!

COKE®—Pharmacist John Pemberton set out to mix up a cure for headaches by mixing coca leaves and cola nuts. Someone in his lab accidentally put some carbonated water into the mixture—and Coca-Cola was launched!

POTATO CHIP—The story goes that George Crum, restaurant owner, was annoyed with a customer who kept complaining that the potatoes coming out of Crum's kitchen were too thick and soggy. Crum sliced the potatoes paper thin and cooked them crisp. Much to his surprise, the customer loved the new form of potatoes.

VELCRO®—On an afternoon hike, Swiss engineer Georges de Mestral found burrs stuck to his dog's fur and to his pants. He noticed that the burrs had hooks that clung to anything with a loop shape. He artificially created the loops and hooks—and crafted a two-sided fastener that could hold all kinds of things together!

Work consulted:
"Top 10 Accidental Inventions." *Famous Scientists & Discoveries @ sciencechannel.* Discovery Communications, n.d. Web. 31 Aug. 2013.

Work consulted:
Cyran, Pamela, and Chris Gaylord. "The 20 most fascinating accidental inventions." *The Christian Science Monitor.* Christian Science Publishing Society, n.d. Web. 30 Aug. 2013.

Did you know that many favorite inventions were the result of happy accidents?

After you enjoy reading about the inventions, answer the questions.

1. Why did the writer choose to organize this piece as eight separate entries?

2. What is the impact of this organization on you as you read?

3. Which invention appealed to you the most? Explain what words, phrases, or ideas led you to this choice.

Name

Copyright © 2014 World Book, Inc./ Incentive Publications, Chicago, IL

Common Core Reinforcement Activities — 7th Grade Language

A GOOD COMBINATION?

Students and cell phones: is this a good combination? You most likely have your own viewpoint on this topic; some people probably agree with you, while others disagree.

Read these three passages about this issue. As you read, look for clues to each author's point of view and purpose for writing the passage.

A

Cell phones should be banned from schools because they are disruptive, unnecessary, and potentially unfair. Students cannot concentrate on learning if ringing and beeping cell phones constantly interrupt them. Cell phones are also disruptive to teachers, particularly if students are playing games or sending text messages during class. If parents need to contact their children during the school day, the school office can pass on a message, so students do not need cell phones during school hours. In addition to being distracting to the learning environment and unnecessary, cell phones could also be used to cheat during class. Even more troubling is the use of cell phones to bully other students at school.

B

Students need to have access to their cell phones throughout the school day and should not be expected to leave their phones in their lockers or cars or, even worse, at home. While cell phones should not be used during class, students must be able to have their cell phones with them in case they need to access their schedules, look up a phone number or address, or make an emergency call. Many students use their cell phones to communicate with their parents during school hours, sharing changes in after-school plans or confirming pick-up times. Banning cell phones from schools essentially forbids student-parent communication during school hours. It is time to move into the 21st century and accept cell phones as an essential part of students' lives.

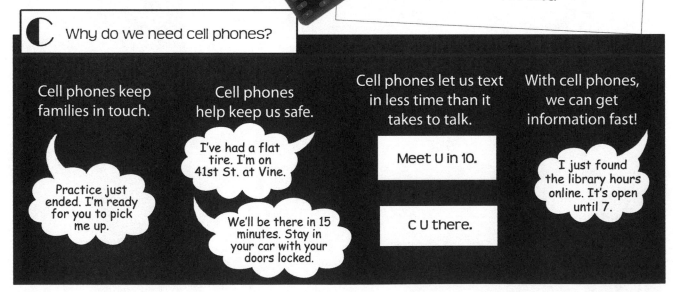

C Why do we need cell phones?

Cell phones keep families in touch.

Practice just ended. I'm ready for you to pick me up.

Cell phones help keep us safe.

I've had a flat tire. I'm on 41st St. at Vine.

We'll be there in 15 minutes. Stay in your car with your doors locked.

Cell phones let us text in less time than it takes to talk.

Meet U in 10.

C U there.

With cell phones, we can get information fast!

I just found the library hours online. It's open until 7.

Name

Use with page 59.

Copyright © 2014 World Book, Inc./ Incentive Publications, Chicago, IL

A GOOD COMBINATION? CONTINUED

Fill in the table below to compare and contrast the three passages.

Cell Phone Passages - Compare and Contrast

	Passage A	Passage B	Passage C
One-sentence summary of the author's point of view or purpose			
Four specific words from the text that reveal the author's position			
One text idea with which you agree			
One text idea with which you disagree			

Which passage do you think makes the best argument?
Explain your answer, using evidence from the text.

Name

Use with page 58.

Copyright © 2014 World Book, Inc./
Incentive Publications, Chicago, IL

ARE YOU CONVINCED?

There are plenty of writers out there in the world with opinions they want to share. Some of them write in the form of an argumentative essay. A good argumentative essay gives evidence, facts, and examples to support a certain point of view or conclusion.

As you read the essay about diving, think about how the writer conveys an opinion. Then use the graphic organizer on the next page to evaluate the essay.

The Dangers of Diving Under Water

Scuba diving offers a unique view of a world that is otherwise not easily accessible. Thousands of people take up the sport each year, eager to see the wonders of life beneath the ocean's surface. But the thrills of this adventure are outweighed by the many risks to human life and health.

Beneath the water, pressure increases by about a half pound per square inch for each foot of depth. If the pressure inside the body is not equal to the outside water pressure, a diver's lungs and other organs can be squeezed and severely injured. This condition is called **barotrauma** or **squeeze.**

While using compressed air from a tank, a diver absorbs considerable amounts of nitrogen into the blood. If a diver ascends to the surface too quickly, bubbles of nitrogen form in the blood and can make the diver ill. This condition is known as **the bends** (decompression sickness) and can be deadly.

Another serious condition, called **air embolism,** can occur during ascent. As a diver rises toward the surface, air in the lungs expands because the air pressure outside the body lessens as the depth of water decreases. This pressure can tear the lungs apart and push air into the bloodstream. This condition can be crippling or deadly.

Another risk is the danger of **oxygen poisoning**. A diver who breathes from a tank that has a high level of oxygen can become very sick or can even die. Some gases at high pressure (such as air in a tank) produce an anesthetic effect called **nitrogen narcosis**. The diver may become drugged or sick.

Of course, in addition to these dangers, there are the risks of accidents, malfunctioning equipment, or attacks by underwater creatures. As you can see, scuba diving is the most dangerous of all sports.

Work consulted:
"Dangers of Scuba Diving" *Scuba Certification*. N.p., 2012. Web. 1 Oct. 2013.

Name

Use with page 61.

60

Copyright © 2014 World Book, Inc./
Incentive Publications, Chicago, IL

ARE YOU CONVINCED? CONTINUED

Complete this organizer to analyze the argument on page 60.

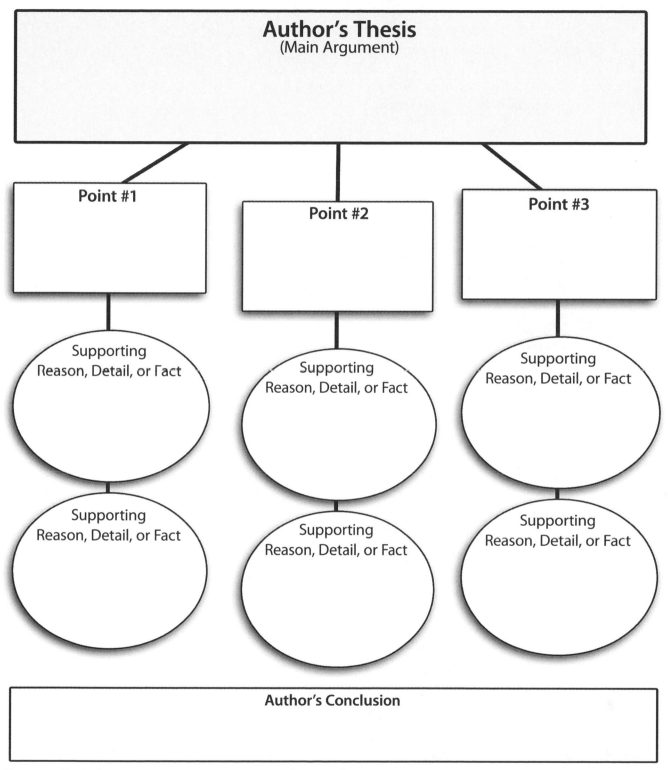

Author's Thesis
(Main Argument)

Point #1

Point #2

Point #3

Supporting
Reason, Detail, or Fact

Supporting
Reason, Detail, or Fact

Supporting
Reason, Detail, or Fact

Supporting
Reason, Detail, or Fact

Supporting
Reason, Detail, or Fact

Supporting
Reason, Detail, or Fact

Author's Conclusion

Do you find this argument convincing? Why or why not?

Name

Use with page 60.

Copyright © 2014 World Book, Inc./
Incentive Publications, Chicago, IL

HIGH-ALTITUDE RUMORS

Many writers or speakers may present information on the same topic. It is almost guaranteed that the presentations will differ—depending on the kind of research, the source of the information, and the choices and style of the writer or speaker. On this page and the next, you will read two passages about the Abominable Snowman.

As you read, think about each author's purpose and how their presentations are different. Answer the questions with each passage.

UH, OH!

You may know this creature as the **Abominable Snowman**—the large ape-like creature that supposedly lives in the high Himalayan Mountains. The local people call him the **Yeti,** which means "little man-like animal" or "troll." Most scientists have concluded that the Yeti does not exist. No pictures have provided evidence. No remains of a Yeti have been found.

Yet, for hundreds of years, natives in the Himalayan Mountains have told stories about an upright primate-like, long-haired creature that roams the mountains. In the 1880s, guides described large footprints left by the Yeti. Reports became more frequent in the twentieth century, with many explorers searching for the Yeti. Interest in this creature increased in 1951 when two British climbers photographed large footprints in the snow on Mt. Everest at about 20,000 feet altitude. Many climbers have reported footprints and sightings of the creature. Others have reported hearing strange calls. One expedition in 1954 found an unidentified ape-like hair, and an Italian mountain climber says he came face to face with a Yeti in 1997. Other strange happenings are unexplained by scientists—especially in places as remote as the cold, high Himalayan Mountains.

The idea of the Abominable Snowman continues to be alive and well and mesmerizing. The Yeti inspires countless movies, books, amusement-park features, rumors, tales, and fireside stories. Certainly something that arouses so much interest and is reported with such frequency must exist.

Work consulted:
Radford, Benjamin. "The Yeti: Asia's Abominable Snowman." *LiveScience.*
Tech Media Network, 27 Nov. 2012. Web. 2 Sept. 2013.

1. How does this author describe the Abominable Snowman?

2. What evidence does this author use to document the creature's existence?

3. What conclusion does the author draw about this creature?

Name

Use with page 63.

Copyright © 2014 World Book, Inc./
Incentive Publications, Chicago, IL

HIGH-ALTITUDE RUMORS, CONTINUED

As you read this second passage, compare it to the first.

4. How does this description of the Yeti or presentation of the information differ from that on page 62?

5. What evidence does this author use to document the creature's existence?

6. What conclusion does this author draw about this creature?

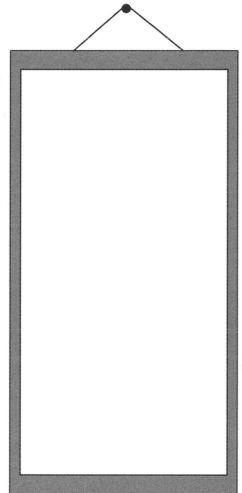

Yeti, also called the *Abominable Snowman,* is a creature said to live on Mount Everest and other mountains of the Himalaya range of Asia. Reports of such a creature have also come from remote parts of China, Siberia, and other parts of Asia. According to legend, the Yeti is a hairy beast with a large, apelike body and a face that resembles that of a human being. It has long arms that reach to its knees, and it walks erect on its thick legs. Legend says that the Yeti sometimes comes down from the mountains to attack villagers.

The name *Abominable Snowman* may have come from a journalist's translation of *metoh kangmi,* a Tibetan name for the creature. The name *Yeti* was given to it by the Sherpa people of Nepal. The word probably once meant *all-devouring creature.* It may refer to a mountain demon rather than a real creature.

There is no direct evidence that the Yeti exists. Local tribes have reported seeing it, but their stories cannot be verified. Since the late 1890's, sightings have been reported by Western travelers, and explorers have sighted footprints of a large, unknown creature in the snow. In 1951, the British explorer Eric Shipton took pictures of "snowman" tracks near Everest. Since then, several expeditions, including one sponsored by World Book in 1960, have searched for the creature. The explorers neither captured nor saw anything that might be the snowman. Scientists of the World Book expedition said the tracks may have been made by bears or other animals. They found that the sun often caused such tracks to melt into large footprints.

In the frame, create a portrait of the Abominable Snowman, or Yeti. Use both authors' descriptions to help you.

Work cited:
Cohen, Daniel. "Yeti." *World Book Student.* World Book, 2013. Web. 16 Sept. 2013.
© World Book, Inc. All rights reserved. Used by permission.

Name

Use with page 62.

LISTEN, WATCH, COMPARE

When you listen to and watch someone deliver a speech, you actually hear and see two things: the content (the information in the speech) and the delivery (how the information is said). In this activity, you will compare reading the speech content with the experience of watching and listening as the same words are delivered by the writer. Look for ways that each impacts you differently.

Well-known poet Nikki Giovanni gave a speech after a tragic shooting at Virginia Tech University. The text of this speech, as well as a video of her delivering the speech, can be found at the following website:

http://www.americanrhetoric.com/speeches/nikkigiovannivatechmemorial.htm
(Please note that Ms. Giovanni's material is protected by copyright.)

A. Read the text of the speech and answer these questions.

1. What parts of the speech text stand out to you when you read them?

2. What do you think is the message of this text?

3. Predict what you think the author will sound like when she delivers this speech. Will it be sad? Passionate? Angry? Solemn? Something else?

How does my delivery affect my message?

B. Watch the video of her delivering the speech. Answer these questions.

4. What surprised you about Ms. Giovanni's delivery of this speech?

5. What parts of the speech stood out to you as you listened and watched?

6. How did the experience of the video presentation affect you differently than reading the speech?

Name

Copyright © 2014 World Book, Inc./ Incentive Publications, Chicago, IL

WRITING

Grade 7

LET ME CONVINCE YOU

The word "argument" might make you think of a dispute between two people, where each is trying to persuade the other that his or her side is the right one.

Argumentative writing has some characteristics similar to such a dispute: there are usually two sides; there are facts, reasons, and examples to support each side; and the goal is to convince the audience that your side is the correct one.

Read these arguments and ask yourself, "Am I convinced? Why or why not?" Then use the next two pages to plan and write your own argument.

Take a Back Seat

The very best seat in a rollercoaster is the last seat. If you want great thrills, run for that last seat.

As the coaster climbs each hill, you have the fun of watching each of the other cars disappear over the edge, and you get the longest time to anticipate the drop.

The last seat is the spot for the greatest speed. As that last car drops over the top, the rollercoaster is going its fastest, and you get the tail end of that tremendous speed.

In the back seat, you also get the longest airtime. This is the time that you fly up out of your seat, feeling weightless because of inertia.

And that's not all the benefits! You get to hear all the screams along the ride as the sounds travel back to you. The ride seems longer, as well, because your car pulls into the station last.

So the next time you ride a coaster, do whatever it takes to get that last seat!

Go for the Front Seat

Run as fast as you can to get in the front seat of the rollercoaster. You'll be glad you did. This is the spot for the greatest thrills. Here, you will feel the greatest force of the wind as the coaster tears down the hills and around corners.

It is only in the front that you can enjoy the unrestricted views and that amazing, terrifying feeling of being utterly alone at the steepest point of the ride.

After the train of cars chug-chug-chugs to the top of the incline, only front riders enjoy that heart-stopping anticipation of dropping over the edge first. There is nothing ahead but empty space and the hope that there is, indeed, a track. With no other humans ahead of you, the most terrified screams you hear are your own.

No other seat in the coaster offers the same combination of dread and excitement.

Name

Use with pages 67 and 68.

Copyright © 2014 World Book, Inc./ Incentive Publications, Chicago, IL

LET ME CONVINCE YOU, CONTINUED

A convincing argument has several important components and takes careful planning. Choose a topic that excites and energizes you!

Fill in the information below to get started.

MIDDLE SCHOOLS SHOULD GIVE MORE HOMEWORK.

SOCIAL NETWORKING MAKES IT HARDER TO HAVE A REAL RELATIONSHIP.

All middle schools should require uniforms.

Argument Planning Guide

What is the main argument you plan to make?

What is your first reason?

What evidence or example supports this reason?

What is your second reason?

What evidence or example supports this reason?

Violent video games make kids more violent.

All pesticides should be banned.

What is your third reason?

What evidence or example supports this reason?

All students should learn a second language.

Football is a safe sport for kids.

Write your concluding statement below. Remember this will be your "last word" to the audience, so make it convincing!

_____

_____

_____

_____

Name _____

Use with pages 66 and 68.

LET ME CONVINCE YOU, CONTINUED

Now use your plan from page 67 to write your argument.
When you're finished, use the checklist while you revise and edit your work.

Argument Checklist

___ My topic sentence clearly introduces my argument.

___ I include reasons and evidence to support my claims.

___ My reasons and evidence are logical, relevant, and accurate.

___ I use transitional words, phrases, and clauses to make my argument flow smoothly.

___ My word choice is appropriate for my audience.

___ My conclusion summarizes my argument clearly and concisely.

___ My spelling, grammar, punctuation, and capitalization are correct.

Now, that should convince everybody!

Name

Use with pages 66 and 67.

Copyright © 2014 World Book, Inc./
Incentive Publications, Chicago, IL

LET ME EXPLAIN

When you write an informative piece, you share knowledge, ideas, or information with your audience.

Read this text to see what you can learn about the topic. Then use the next two pages to plan and write a "how-to" explanation of your own.

How to Spit a Cricket in Competition

Yes! People actually do this—place a cricket in the mouth and spit to see how far it can fly! You can do this too!

First, you'll have to sign up for a cricket-spitting competition. Look on the Internet to find the closest one to your home. You'll probably want to practice a lot too. Each competition has its own rules, but the procedures are similar. Learn the rules for your competition.

Some good news is that you don't have to bring your own crickets. Crickets are frozen and slightly thawed when it's time for the spitting. Usually each competitor is offered a selection of two or three crickets from which to choose. All crickets must be intact—with all six legs, four wings, and two antennae in place—before being spit.

Place the cricket (dead, of course) in the center of your tongue near the front. The bug must be entirely in your mouth with no part of it showing before you can enter the cricket-spitting circle. You must spit the cricket within 20 seconds of entering the ring. Take a deep breath, being careful not to swallow the insect. Exhale as hard as you can—just as if you were spitting out a watermelon seed. Spit the cricket as far as you can.

When you practice, measure the distances and keep a record of your tries. If you practice enough, maybe you can beat the world record. Dan Capps of Wisconsin is the current Guinness World Champion cricket spitter. He set the record in 1998 with a spitting distance of 32 feet and 5 inches. Isn't it about time you got busy and broke that record?

Work consulted:
Axson, Scooby. "Our Unnatural Pastime: Cricket Spitting." *Columbia News Service.*
Columbia University, Mar. 2012. Web. 5 Sept 2013.

How to keep your locker clean • How to kick a soccer ball • HOW TO DO A CARTWHEEL
How to make a perfect turkey sandwich • How to train your puppy • How to Make Spaghetti
HOW TO HOLD A GREAT BIRTHDAY PARTY • How to choose a friend

Name

Use with pages 70 and 71.

LET ME EXPLAIN, CONTINUED

"How-To" Planning Guide

What are you going to explain or teach others how to do?

How will you introduce the topic in a way that will get the audience's attention?

How will you organize your information? Do the steps need to be in a specific order?

List a few things that you know how to do well.

_____

_____

_____

_____

_____

_____

Put a star by one that you can turn into "how-to" informative writing.

What details, facts, and examples will you include?

What special vocabulary will you need to use?

Will you need to include a graphic (like a chart or a picture) to help your reader understand? If so, what will it look like and what information will it contain?

How will you conclude your piece in a way that helps your audience reflect on the information you've given?

_____

_____

_____

Name

Use with pages 69 and 71.

Copyright © 2014 World Book, Inc./
Incentive Publications, Chicago, IL

LET ME EXPLAIN, CONTINUED

Now use your plan from page 70 to write your "how-to" piece.
When you're finished, use the checklist while you revise and edit your work.

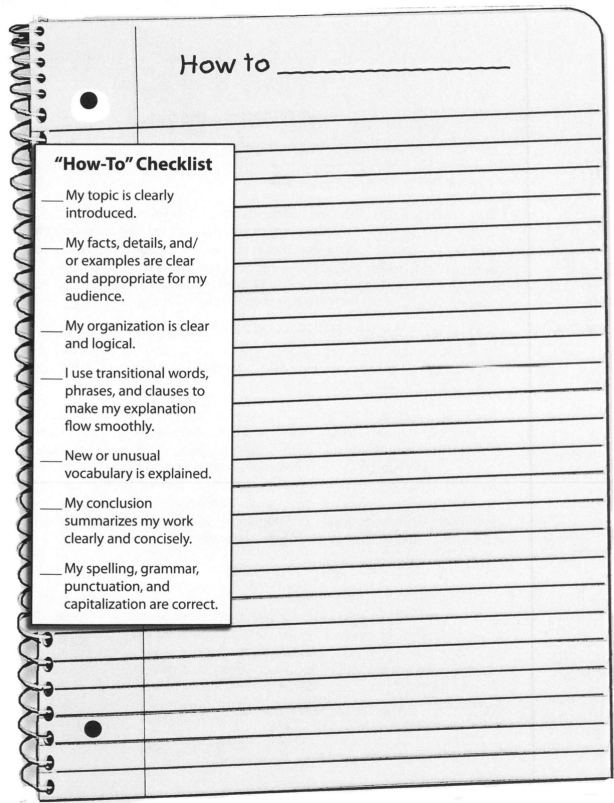

How to _____

"How-To" Checklist

___ My topic is clearly introduced.

___ My facts, details, and/ or examples are clear and appropriate for my audience.

___ My organization is clear and logical.

___ I use transitional words, phrases, and clauses to make my explanation flow smoothly.

___ New or unusual vocabulary is explained.

___ My conclusion summarizes my work clearly and concisely.

___ My spelling, grammar, punctuation, and capitalization are correct.

Name

Use with pages 69 and 70.

Copyright © 2014 World Book, Inc./
Incentive Publications, Chicago, IL

Common Core Reinforcement Activities — 7th Grade Language

LET ME TELL YOU A STORY

A narrative is a story, whether true or imagined. A good narrative has a setting, a plot, interesting characters, and descriptive details. Depending on the story's topic and mood, and the tone, it may also include such things as suspense, humor, adventure, or love.

Read the story below and try to picture the events in your mind as they unfold. Then use the next two pages to plan and write your own story.

Trouble Falls from the Sky

The urgent call came into the Discreet Inquiries Detective Agency at exactly 6:30 P.M. "Help! Mice! Mice are everywhere! They are falling from the sky! My business is ruined!" screamed the agitated caller.

Detective C.C. Sharp calmed the troubled restaurant owner just enough to get the story. In fits and gasps, Chef Patrice managed to tell the tale. At the height of the busy dinner hour at the elegant Les Manages restaurant, dozens of mice parachuted down from the sky. A red shoelace fastened a tiny parachute to each mouse. Squealing rodents landed on the outdoor dining patio, then began scampering around the floor and across the tables.

Les Manages, it turns out, is located next to the Claws & Paws Pet Shop. Restaurant owner Patrice interrupted her panicked description to explain that she had recently filed a lawsuit against the pet shop claiming that the shop's odors drove customers away from the restaurant.

Then Patrice went back to frenetically recounting the incident. "They came out of nowhere. We heard no airplanes. No one saw anything overhead. I was just serving an Anjou pear crème brulee to a large group of guests. All of a sudden, at least a hundred tiny red parachutes were floating down. We heard squeaking. Then they landed. One mouse plopped right into a customer's dessert. Another got tangled in the top-knot chignon of the mayor's wife. Those nasty little creatures scattered everywhere nibbling on appetizers, stepping in salads, and even gnawing *tournedos de boeuf*. All my guests ran away screaming."

Pacing and waving her arms, Patrice gave one last plea: "What shall I do? No one will ever come to Les Manages again! What am I to do?"

Working hard to keep from smiling at the vision of the clever prank, Detective Sharp assured Patrice that the police would have no trouble getting to the bottom of this mystery. An arrest was made within hours. Better yet, Patrice's worries were for naught. Customers and staff members at the site had posted and tweeted pictures on social network sites. The story went viral. In a matter of days, customers from cities near and far were flocking to Les Manages in hopes of dining among parachuting mice.

LET ME TELL YOU A STORY, CONTINUED

For your own narrative, tell a story about your best day ever. It can be a day that really happened to you or what you imagine your best day ever would be.

Use the planning guide to get ready for your writing. Remember to think about the sensory details—sights, sounds, smells, tastes—when making your plan.

Narrative Planning Guide

How will your tale begin?

Will this story be told from the first-person or third-person point of view? How will this point of view be introduced?

What details will you use to establish the setting?

How will you introduce the narrator and the characters? Will there be dialogue in your story?

How will your story be organized so that it's logical and makes sense to the reader?

What details will you include to help your reader picture the events?

How will you end the story?

Jot down some ideas about your best day ever.

Be sure to answer these questions as you plan:

Where was it?

When did it happen?

Who was with me?

What happened?

How did it end?

What did I learn?

Ah, that was
a really great day!

Name

Use with pages 72 and 74.

LET ME TELL YOU A STORY, CONTINUED

Now use your plan from page 73 to write your story! Use the blank oval to add a cartoon, diagram, or other visual to accompany the story. When you're finished, use the checklist while you revise and edit your work.

_____

_____

_____

_____

_____

_____

_____

_____

_____

_____

_____

_____

_____

_____

_____

Narrative Checklist

___ The beginning of my story grabs the audience's attention and makes them want to read more.

___ The events unfold naturally and logically.

___ The characters, including the narrator, are well developed and interesting.

___ I use a variety of words and sentence structures to engage my audience.

___ I include relevant descriptive details and sensory language.

___ Transitions make my sentences flow smoothly and keep the action moving.

___ My story has a conclusion that summarizes up and/or reflects on the events of my best day ever.

___ My spelling, grammar, punctuation, and capitalization are correct (including punctuating dialogue).

Name

Use with pages 72 and 73.

Copyright © 2014 World Book, Inc./ Incentive Publications, Chicago, IL

SENSE-ABLE WORD CHOICES

A writer's job is to affect the reader powerfully. The more sad, happy, satisfied, angry, annoyed, explosive, excited (or so on) the reader's reaction to the piece, the more successful the writing!!

One effective way to evoke a strong response in a reader is to assault his or her senses with the vivid images. These can awaken any one or more of the reader's senses: touch, taste, smell, sight, or hearing. To ignite a strong response, you'll need to use precise and compelling words.

Practice effective word choice.
Begin by circling the best word or phrase choice for each example:

1. A (bad, putrid) odor rose from the garbage can.

2. (Slimy, Wet) globs of rotten pudding (flowed, oozed) along the ground.

3. I choked on the (thick, curdled) fumes blowing through the alley.

Choose a new topic for your writing. _____

Write at least eight words or phrases that you could use in a description. Avoid the most ordinary words. Choose words that will stimulate the reader's senses. On a separate sheet of paper, use some of your words and phrases to write a short description, poem, or other piece that creates a strong, sensory experience for your reader.

Name

Copyright © 2014 World Book, Inc./
Incentive Publications, Chicago, IL

Common Core Reinforcement Activities — 7th Grade Language

COMBINE AND REALIGN

Sometimes a short, abrupt sentence can make the perfect statement. On other occasions, a longer, more complex sentence best expresses what you want to say. It is difficult to write a piece that has an appealing combination of sentence length and structure. Sometimes ideas need to be moved around, combined, and realigned.

On this page and the next are four groups of short, choppy sentences. Choose at least two of these to practice your skills. Rearrange, realign, and combine the sentences as needed to form a well-composed paragraph of varying sentence lengths. Your paragraph should flow smoothly and engage the reader. Feel free to change the sequence, delete words, or add connecting words. Write your new versions on a separate piece of paper.

I have a cat.

Her name is Lacy Daisy.

That's because she is unquestionably feminine.

She also likes long, leisurely siestas.

She sips, rather than laps milk.

She tilts her head saucily.

She expects to be pampered.

She thinks she's a princess.

I love her.

Storms are scary.
They announce themselves in different ways.
Tornadoes are so sudden.
You have little time to prepare.
You can't defend yourself.
You can know too far ahead of time about a storm.
Hurricanes come slowly.
Then you have to worry longer.
You can see rainstorms boiling up in the distance.
Then they roar in on a thunderbolt.
They can come slow or fast.
However a storm arrives, I get extremely nervous.
I wish they could be stopped somehow.
I'd like to make a law against them.
I'd stamp them "Canceled!"
I would click them off like a TV.
I can't control nature.
Nature is a lot like life.
You just have to let it happen.

Name

Use with page 77.

Copyright © 2014 World Book, Inc./
Incentive Publications, Chicago, IL

COMBINE AND REALIGN, CONTINUED

Saturday was a bummer.
It was raining.
The telephone rang at 6:00 A.M.
No one was up.
It was a wrong number.
Good grief!
The toilet wouldn't flush.
The top had been left off the garbage.
The dog dragged the trash all over the yard.
A bird flew into the window.
The window cracked.
My father swore.
My mother cried.
I forgot my piano lesson was changed—to Tuesday.
I rode my bike six blocks in the rain before
  I remembered.
I dropped my phone in a puddle.
I missed a call.
It was from a girl.
She'll probably never call again.
I ate cold pizza for lunch.
It was gross.
I went back to bed.

I broke up with my boyfriend today.
Well, that's not exactly true.
He broke up with me.
I didn't want this.
It wasn't my choice.
Jana told me that Brad told her.
Jesse told Brad that Mike was getting tired of me.
But Mike told Jesse not to tell anyone.
And Jesse told Brad not to tell that he told.
Brad told Jana he'd kill her if she told me.
But she did.
I asked Mike if it was true
I prayed he'd say, "No."
But he said, "Yes."
Well, he's a jerk anyway.

Name

Use with page 76.

MULTIFARIOUS FORMS

A writer's message may be delivered to a reader in multifarious (look it up) forms! One simple idea can be written as a slogan, a song, a poster, a story, a chant, a speech, a letter, or a rhyme. A sample idea is expressed below in a variety of forms.

Identify a wish or dream you have, and express your idea in as many different forms of writing as possible. Use your own paper, stationery, posters, or other materials to do your writing.

SAMPLE IDEA — I wish I had a horse!

A horse! My kingdom for a horse!

a play

"Richard III" by Wm. Shakespeare

a want ad

WANTED:
Equine beast of excellent quality. Royal lineage preferred over brawn or speed. Contact I. Thackery at Brighton Eaves, Cornwall.

a poem

Oh, how I wish I had a horse,
A beast of elegant stature, of course—
Not the drudge of a farmer's land
Or a racer trained by a jockey's hand,
But a steed who is spirited, fearless, and free—
A powerful creature of majesty!
But should my magical equine dream
Melt like a dollop of sweet ice cream
In the heat of harsh reality,
I'll have any beast of fair quality!

a tongue twister

The speedy steed supersedes the speed of a velocipede!

a letter

Captain of the Horse Guard
Her Majesty's Royalty Stables
Kensington Palace, London
9 October

Dear Sir,
I am writing to inquire whether you might be acquainted with a horse of elegant stature who may have proved a bit spirited for the rigorous formal duties of the horse guard and is therefore available for purchase. If so, please respond to 31 W. Brighton Eaves, Cornwall. Eagerly and humbly awaiting your kind response.

Your fellow equestrian,
Ian Thackery

Name

Copyright © 2014 World Book, Inc./ Incentive Publications, Chicago, IL

THAT'S A GOOD QUESTION!

You may not realize it, but you conduct some type of research every day. You may be answering simple questions like, "What time does the movie start?" or "How much will those new shoes cost?" Or you may need to research more complex questions like, "What kind of exercises should I do to improve my basketball skills?"

Effective research writing involves consulting several reliable sources, paraphrasing or quoting appropriate information, and presenting conclusions clearly and concisely. Here is a sample of research writing that answers the question, "Why do onions make you cry?"

"Why do onions make you cry?"

If you've ever chopped an onion, you know that it can bring tears to your eyes no matter what mood you're in! Why do onions make people cry? The answer has to do with a chemical reaction between the enzymes in the onion, the air, and your own tears. When you cut an onion, you break apart the cells inside, allowing their enzymes to mix with the air. The resulting gas, called syn-propanethial-S-oxide, mixes with tears to form sulfuric acid. The acid is very irritating to the eyes and makes them burn. In response, your eyes make lots of tears to flush out the acid. So whether you love onions or hate them, you can expect to cry when it's time to chop them up!

Works consulted:
Helemenstine, Anne Marie. "Why Do Onions Make You Cry?" *About.com Chemistry.*
The New York Times, n.d. Web. 16 Sept. 2013.
"Why Does Chopping an Onion Make You Cry?" *Everyday Mysteries.* Library of
Congress, Aug. 2010. Web. 16 Sept 2013.

Here are some other science-related questions you may want to research:

- What animals can re-grow damaged body parts?
- How does a chick breathe inside a shell?
- Why are moths drawn to lights?
- Do fish really have short memories?
- Could extinct species be brought back to life?
- Why do some fruits turn brown when they're cut open?
- Why do some people go bald?
- How do bees communicate with each other?
- Why do your ears pop when you fly on a plane?

Name

Use with pages 80 and 81.

THAT'S A GOOD QUESTION!, CONTINUED

????? ???? ?? ??? ????? ?????? ??? ????? ??? ??? ?????? ?? ?

What is your question? _____

Fill in the table as you research. Use your classroom style guide for citations.

PARAPHRASE OR QUOTE OF DATA OR INFORMATION	SOURCES YOU WILL CONSULT AND CITE	ASSESSMENT OF SOURCE CREDIBILITY AND ACCURACY

What other questions were raised as you pursued this one?

Name

Use with pages 79 and 81.

Copyright © 2014 World Book, Inc./ Incentive Publications, Chicago, IL

THAT'S A GOOD QUESTION!, CONTINUED

Now it's your turn to share what you learned. Use the lines to present your conclusions in a well-organized paragraph or two. Then use the oval to add an illustration or other graphic to add interest to your writing. Cite (give credit to) your sources and consult the checklist while you revise and edit your work.

Research-Writing Checklist

____ My topic sentence refers to my original question.

____ My information includes evidence from multiple reliable sources.

____ I paraphrase or use quotations when needed AND cite the original source(s).

____ My ideas flow smoothly and are well organized.

____ My conclusion summarizes my ideas and makes my audience think.

____ My spelling, grammar, punctuation, and capitalization are correct.

Name _____

Use with pages 79 and 80.

Copyright © 2014 World Book, Inc./
Incentive Publications, Chicago, IL

Common Core Reinforcement Activities — 7th Grade Language

FIGURATIVELY SPEAKING

The fireworks have begun their show.

So catch your breath and hold your ears.

Drops of turquoise give the night a fresh shower

And pretty-patterned purples paint a dark canvas.

Sharp crimson spikes shoot like arrows.

Glistening golds glitter

While blasts of blues burst into the blackness.

Fuchsia fragments fling themselves,

Chasing after twinkling chartreuse puffballs.

Yellows sparkle, stretching their wiggly fingers out

To claw at the skies.

The silence is split by cracks and pops.

Confetti explosions roar and clatter,

Shattering the night.

BOOM!

crackle...

Pop!

**After carefully reading
the "painted" poem, follow these directions:**

1. Underline three examples of alliteration in the poem.

2. Circle two examples of onomatopoeia.

3. Put a star next to a line that uses personification.

4. Put a box around one simile.

5. How does the visual layout of the poem contribute to the message of the poem?

6. What other topics would lend themselves to this same structure?

Name

Use with page 83.

Copyright © 2014 World Book, Inc./
Incentive Publications, Chicago, IL

FIGURATIVELY SPEAKING, CONTINUED

Using the poem and your responses on page 82, write a well organized paragraph addressing this question: **What impact does the poet's use of figurative language (alliteration, onomatopoeia, personification, simile) have on the effect of "Fireworks"?**

Include at least three direct quotes from the poem to illustrate your answer. When you're finished, use the checklist while you revise and edit your work.

_____

_____

_____

_____

_____

_____

_____

_____

_____

_____

_____

_____

_____

_____

_____

_____

Poetry-Analysis Checklist

__ My response directly answers the question above.

__ I include at least one quote from the poem to strengthen my point.

__ My ideas flow smoothly and are well organized.

__ My response ends with a thoughtful conclusion.

__ My spelling, grammar, punctuation, and capitalization are correct.

Name _____

Use with page 82.

SCRUTINIZE AND SUMMARIZE

Summarizing what you read is a way to condense information and focus on the most important points.

As you read this passage, watch for the central ideas.

Kicking is the most important skill in soccer. It involves shooting at the goal, putting the ball in play, or putting the ball into a particular area of the field. A good player can kick the ball accurately in many ways with either foot.

In most cases, kicking the ball with the instep is the most effective method. A player can control the accuracy, distance, and power of a kick better with the instep than in any other way. In certain situations, however, a player might use the outer or inner side of the foot or even the heel.

Soccer players generally try to kick the ball so that it travels just above the field. Players put their nonkicking foot next to the ball. They keep their head down and their eyes on the ball. Then they swing their kicking leg with the toes pointed downward and kick the ball squarely with the instep. After the foot strikes the ball, the leg should straighten and follow through. This action makes the ball travel in the right direction.

A player usually stops the ball before kicking it. Kicking a moving ball lessens the player's control over the direction of the kick.

Work cited:
Applegate, David M. " Soccer." *World Book Student*. World Book, 2013. Web. 2 Sept. 2013.
© World Book, Inc. All rights reserved. Used by permission.

Now try this: summarize the main points of this passage in exactly 15 words:

_____ _____

_____ _____

_____ _____

_____ _____

_____ _____

_____ _____

_____ _____

_____

Name

SPEAKING AND LISTENING

Grade 7

COLLABORATOR'S GUIDE

There are many times in school and beyond when you will need to collaborate with other people. You may be working together to complete a project, make a decision, discuss a book, or accomplish some other goal.

No matter the situation, there are four words that will make your collaboration the best it can be: **prepare**, **listen**, **respect**, and **respond**. Here are some guidelines to get you started. Have your group add their own ideas, too.

I researched facts about our topic and made notes for the group.

Prepare
- Be sure you understand the task.
- Know your role in the group.
- Research your topic.

I listen and pay close attention to the opinions of my group.

Sometimes I respectfully disagree . . . .

. . . but most of the time I give them a thumbs up!

Listen
- Pay attention to what your group members are saying.
- Have an open mind.
- Use encouraging body language.

Respect
- Look at people as they speak.
- Don't belittle anyone else's comments or answers.
- Don't interrupt or get distracted.

Some of Josh's points needed clarification, but overall, his presentation was very persuasive!

Respond
- Express your views clearly.
- If you don't understand something, ask clarifying questions.
- Give positive feedback when appropriate.

Name

Copyright © 2014 World Book, Inc./ Incentive Publications, Chicago, IL

COLLABORATOR'S GUIDE: PREPARE!

Any group collaboration will be more successful if members are prepared!

Use this checklist to get ready for your discussion. Then fill out the *I'm Prepared!* form before you begin.

I'm Prepared!

Collaborator's Checklist

____ Be sure you understand the assignment and the goal(s) of the discussion.

____ Know how your discussion and its outcomes will be evaluated. (For example, ask yourself, "What are the expectations? What is the assignment?")

____ Do some research on any aspect of the discussion you don't understand or about which you have questions.

____ Prepare some questions you could ask other group members to keep the discussion going. Avoid questions that can be answered "yes" or "no."

____ Set one or two reasonable goals for yourself in the discussion. How many times will you participate? Will you work on your eye contact, on not interrupting, or on drawing others into the discussion?

Group Discussion Task:

What I have done to prepare:

Evidence I will contribute:

Questions I will ask:

My sources:

I've reviewed the rules for collaboration: ____

Name _____

Copyright © 2014 World Book, Inc./
Incentive Publications, Chicago, IL

COLLABORATOR'S GUIDE:
LISTEN, RESPECT, RESPOND

During a discussion, it is important that the group stays focused on the goals and every member contributes. One way to accomplish this is to have one group member serve as a recorder, making tally marks or notes on a chart, as the discussion progresses.

Before the discussion, fill in this information:

Group members and their roles:

Discussion topic, question, issue, or task:

Goals and deadline:

During the discussion, keep track of members' participation on the chart.

NAME OF GROUP MEMBER	CONTRIBUTED NEW INFORMATION	ASKED A QUESTION	BROUGHT A NEW MEMBER INTO THE DISCUSSION	ACKNOWLEDGED NEW INFORMATION	BROUGHT THE DISCUSSION BACK ON TRACK
(example) Bob	////	//		//	/

After the discussion, answer these questions as a group:

What aspects of the discussion did our group do well?

What aspects do we need to work on next time?

Did we accomplish our task or goal?

Name

Copyright © 2014 World Book, Inc./ Incentive Publications, Chicago, IL

COLLABORATOR'S GUIDE: REFLECT

After your discussion, it is always helpful to think about how you did.

Look over the chart from page 88 for your group and fill in the speech bubbles below:

Was your preparation good enough to help the group?

What was your most important contribution to the group?

What part of "Listen, Respect, Respond" did you do best?

What are two things you learned from this discussion?

What do you need to do better next time?

What is your opinion of this discussion overall? Why?

Name

Copyright © 2014 World Book, Inc./
Incentive Publications, Chicago, IL

Common Core Reinforcement Activities — 7th Grade Language

LISTENER'S GUIDE

We are bombarded by sounds every day: people talking, car engines roaring, dogs barking, phones ringing, and many more. But what happens when you need to get *information* from something you hear—such as a video, a lecture, or a demonstration? What's the difference between just hearing something and **really listening?**

Listening is active. That means you have to do more than just hear the sounds; you have to use your brain to make sense of what you're hearing. You may also have to summarize ideas as you hear them or take notes to help you remember what you've heard. Here is a guide to help you become a great listener.

1. Anticipate what you're going to hear and what information you want to get so your brain can be ready. "What's the topic? Who is speaking? Who is the intended audience? What am I supposed to learn?"

2. Stay focused on the task and avoid distractions.

3. Listen for main points and details.

I'm listening!

4. Look for patterns in the information— does the speaker repeat important points? Or use certain body language to emphasize a point?

5. Watch for any visual aids or demonstrations that enhance the information.

6. Repeat important facts inside your head after you hear them.

7. Take notes if possible.

8. Write down any questions you have while they're fresh in your mind.

9. Be prepared to summarize what you've heard.

10. Be able to explain what you learned and how it helped you learn a new topic or clarify something you already knew.

Name

Copyright © 2014 World Book, Inc./ Incentive Publications, Chicago, IL

I LISTENED! I WATCHED! I LEARNED!

Use this form to respond to what you heard in any oral presentation.

Presentation Response Form

The main purpose of this presentation was...

The main idea was...

　　　　Details or examples that supported the main idea were...

Another key idea was...

　　　　Details or examples that supported this idea were...

How was the information presented?

What specific things about the presentation helped you learn something new? (Explain your answer.)

What specific things about the presentation helped you clarify a topic or issue you already knew something about? (Explain your answer.)

Thought provoking!

What nonspoken components added to the message and what did they add?

What did you learn from this presentation?

Name

Copyright © 2014 World Book, Inc./
Incentive Publications, Chicago, IL

Common Core Reinforcement Activities — 7th Grade Language

SURROUNDED BY OPPOSITES:
A LISTENING TASK

To the teacher: Use this story and the accompanying graphic as a listening task. Read the story or choose another reader to present it. Provide students with the illustration by projecting it or supplying it in print form to each student (but delete the other text from the page). Students can complete the *Presentation Response Form* on page 91 after listening to the passage.

About a week ago, the strangeness of it all settled in on Samatha. Something was wrong. Signs told her to do things that contradicted what she thought she should do. Friends made suggestions that conflicted with their previous advice. Dinner replaced breakfast. Teachers collected homework at the ends of classes.

When Mom scolded her, "Getting your homework in on time was despicable!" Sam's concern doubled. When she got home late from a party, she knew that trouble would follow. But her dad hollered, "Hey Sam, you'll never have a curfew again!" Her worries multiplied a thousand times.

When Saturday arrived, Samantha longed for a break from the confusion. Hoping to relieve her stress, she gathered up her favorite books and headed for the beach.

Alas! Relief was nowhere in sight.

Name

Copyright © 2014 World Book, Inc./ Incentive Publications, Chicago, IL

I HEAR YOU

There are many people out there trying to convince you about a variety of topics: politicians, advertisers, salespeople, and even friends. Learning to listen carefully to an argumentative presentation is a vital skill that will help you make decisions for yourself.

These questions will help you listen carefully and evaluate the argument for yourself. Take notes as you listen.

What is the speaker's topic?

What argument is the speaker making about this topic?

What claims does the speaker make to back up the argument? (For each claim, ask yourself the following: "Was the reasoning logical?" "Was the claim relevant to the argument?" "Was there reliable evidence to back up the claim?" "Was there enough evidence to persuade you?")

Were you left with unanswered questions? If so, what are they?

All students should learn to play a musical instrument.

Junk food should have higher taxes to encourage healthier eating.

Zoos should be outlawed.

The voting age should be lowered.

Television is more instructive than books.

Homework does more harm than good.

All cars should run on electrical power.

Schools should eliminate letter grades.

Reality television is harmful.

Schools should ban soda machines.

Vampire shows are harmful to kids.

Tattoos are safe.

Peers have more influence on teens than parents.

Name

REFLECTION ON AN ARGUMENT

After listening to and evaluating an argument, it is important to reflect on what you heard, what you learned, and whether or not you were persuaded.

Use this graphic organizer to reflect on a speech you have heard.
Use any notes you took on the previous page.

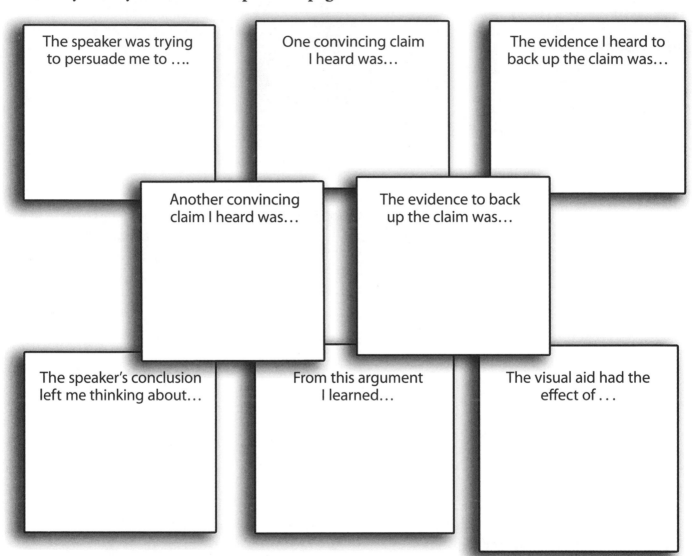

The speaker was trying to persuade me to ….

One convincing claim I heard was…

The evidence I heard to back up the claim was…

Another convincing claim I heard was…

The evidence to back up the claim was…

The speaker's conclusion left me thinking about…

From this argument I learned…

The visual aid had the effect of . . .

Use the scale to rate each item below, with 1 being low and 5 being high.

Overall the speaker's reasoning was sound.   1   2   3   4   5

The speaker had enough evidence.   1   2   3   4   5

The speaker persuaded me.   1   2   3   4   5

Name

Copyright © 2014 World Book, Inc./ Incentive Publications, Chicago, IL

SPEAKER'S GUIDE

Every great speech has two important components: **content**, or what you say, and **delivery**, or how you say it. Both of these components work together to make an impact on your audience.

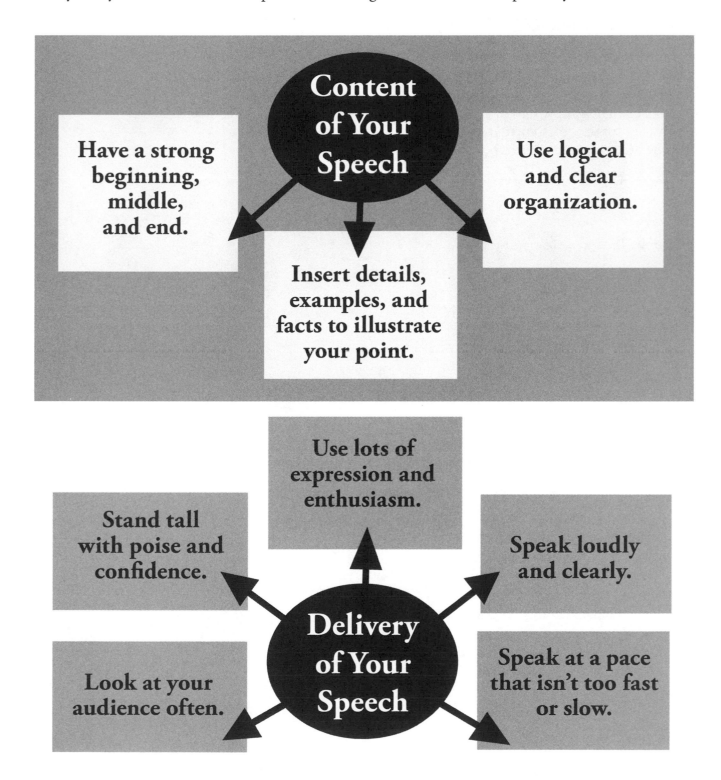

PLANNING A GREAT SPEECH

This activity is designed to help everyone get to know each other and begin to feel comfortable speaking in front of the class.

Here's how it works:

Choose a classmate you don't already know (or your teacher may assign a partner) and interview him or her! Below are some topics you can ask about. You can also add your own.

hobbies & interests

pets   sports

foods you love or hate

family   adventures

characteristics & talents

favorite books & movies

music   dreams   goals

Be a good interviewer! Go wherever the conversation takes you!

Use the space on the right to take notes as you interview.

When you feel you have enough information for a great speech, decide how you will organize it and transfer some notes onto a note card to use during your speech. Remember to think about a strong beginning, middle, and end.

Then **PRACTICE!** Use the *How Was the Speech?* form on page 98 to guide you as you prepare.

When it's your turn, you and your partner will go to the front of the class and give your introductions. You will each speak about each other, one at a time.

Name

Copyright © 2014 World Book, Inc./
Incentive Publications, Chicago, IL

REFLECTING ON MY SPEECH

Answer the following questions in complete sentences.

Speech topic or title: Date:

- **What part** of this speech assignment was the easiest for you? (Think about interviewing, organizing, giving the speech, etc.) Explain your answer.

- **What part** of this asssignment was the most difficult for you? Explain your answer.

- **What part** of your speech leaves you feeling the most proud? Why?

- **What two** areas do you need to improve when you make speeches in the future?

  1.

  2.

- **What is one thing** you learned from this speech assignment?

Name

Copyright © 2014 World Book, Inc./
Incentive Publications, Chicago, IL

Common Core Reinforcement Activities — 7th Grade Language

HOW WAS THE SPEECH?

Use this form (including the scale at the bottom of the page) to evaluate each other's speeches. Be sure to include comments and suggestions.

Speaker: _____ **Date:** _____

Topic or Assignment: _____

Content *(What was said?)*

Introduction	1	2	3	4	5
Body					
Clear identification of facts	1	2	3	4	5
Appropriate details	1	2	3	4	5
Organization	1	2	3	4	5
Conclusion	1	2	3	4	5

Delivery *(How was it said?)*

Confidence and poise	1	2	3	4	5
Eye contact	1	2	3	4	5
Volume and clarity	1	2	3	4	5
Pace	1	2	3	4	5
Expression and enthusiasm	1	2	3	4	5

Comments and suggestions for the speaker:

Scale

5 points = Excellent! No improvements needed.

4 points = Very good. Only a little improvement needed.

3 points = Average. More practice required.

2 points = Below average or barely evident. Needs more work.

1 point = Poor or missing. Needs lots of work!

Name _____

LANGUAGE

Grade 7

ON THE RECORD

A **phrase** is a group of related words that lacks either a subject or a predicate (or both). Phrases usually take their names from the main words that introduce them (prepositional phrase, verb phrase, noun phrase). They can be used as subjects, objects, nouns, or modifiers.

A. Circle the phrases in these sentences. For each phrase you find, be ready to describe its function in the sentence.

1. The reporter conducting the interview has often worked in this location.

2. Learning to talk to animals is something Ms. Lewis studies in night school.

3. Those fish with the long bodies, huge jaws, and sharp teeth are barracudas.

4. That great barracuda preying on other sea creatures is called the "tiger of the sea."

B. Write two or three sentences about Mr. Barracuda. Include several phrases and circle them as you go.

_____

_____

_____

_____

_____

Name

A WHALE OF A TALE

A clause is a group of related words that has both a subject and a verb. Some (independent clauses) express complete thoughts and can stand alone. Others (dependent clauses) cannot stand alone. Dependent clauses begin with either a subordinating conjunction (such as *after, although, because, before* or *if*) or a relative pronoun (such as *who, whose, which* or *that*). A dependent clause can be used as a subject, object, predicate noun, or modifier.

This tale about a whale is loaded with clauses.
(Most tales are!) Can you find them all?

A. Circle the clauses in these sentences. For each clause you find, be ready to describe its function in the sentence.

1. The large whale, which was caught up in a storm, washed ashore in the waves.

2. A crowd gathered around the whale, worried that the whale might perish on the beach.

3. Scientists enlisted whoever was on the beach to help save the mammal.

4. Because the whale's survival depended on staying hydrated, biologists kept the animal wet as they examined it.

5. The people on the beach who encouraged the whale and helped keep her wet watched the animal return to its ocean home.

6. That the whale tipped her tail toward the beach delighted her cheering landlubber friends.

B. Follow the directions to complete each sentence.

7. Write an adjective clause that describes the whale.
   The whale _____ was awe inspiring!

8. Write a noun clause that is the subject of the sentence.
   _____ is that the whale will join her friends at sea.

Name _____

Copyright © 2014 World Book, Inc. /
Incentive Publications, Chicago, IL

Common Core Reinforcement Activities — 7th Grade Language

EXCEPTIONAL SENTENCES

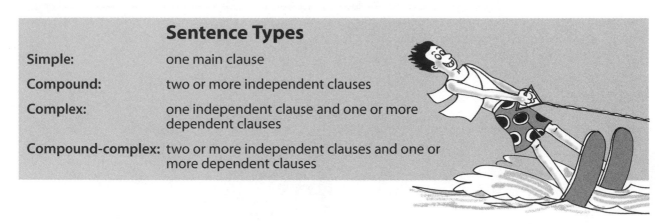

Sentence Types

Simple:	one main clause
Compound:	two or more independent clauses
Complex:	one independent clause and one or more dependent clauses
Compound-complex:	two or more independent clauses and one or more dependent clauses

Keep tales of your adventures engaging by mixing up the kinds of sentences you use.

Label each sentence type with S (simple), C (compound), CX (complex), or CC (compound-complex).

_____ 1. The first time I water-skied, I discovered it was much harder than I thought!

_____ 2. I sat in the water ready to go, and I watched my uncle start the boat.

_____ 3. As the boat accelerated, I put my weight on my skis, I leaned forward, and I tried to stand up.

_____ 4. Before I could stand up, I found myself face down in the water.

_____ 5. Clearly, this wasn't how it was supposed to go!

_____ 6. I refused to give up, so I tried again.

_____ 7. With a little practice, I was finally able to stay on my feet.

_____ 8. I stayed on my skis for about thirty seconds until my arms gave out.

_____ 9. It was exhausting but exhilarating!

_____ 10. Ever since that day, I go water-skiing whenever I can!

_____ 11. Would you like me to teach you to ski?

Name _____

Copyright © 2014 World Book, Inc./
Incentive Publications, Chicago, IL

CREATE EIGHT!

Imagine what an octopus would say if he (or she) could express ideas, observations, or opinions—or have a conversation with another octopus!

In each speech balloon, write a statement or question of the type to fit the label (S for simple, C for compound, CX for complex, or CC for compound-complex).

1. (S)

2. (CC)

3. (C)

4. (CC)

5. (S)

6. (S)

7. (CC)

8. (CX)

9. (C)

10. (CC)

Name

Copyright © 2014 World Book, Inc./
Incentive Publications, Chicago, IL

Common Core Reinforcement Activities — 7th Grade Language

NO DANGLING, PLEASE

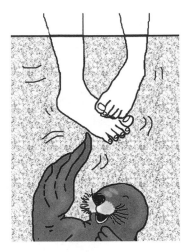

If a modifying clause or phrase does not clearly and sensibly modify a word in the sentence, or if it is not placed close to the word it modifies, it is called a *dangling modifier* or a *misplaced modifier*. Misplaced modifiers confuse the meaning of the sentence.

Crabs were served to the guests *covered with butter.*

It's not a good idea to dangle your feet off the pier unless you're sure about what's lurking below the surface of the water. Also, it's not a good idea to dangle modifiers in sentences.

Rewrite each sentence to straighten out the misplaced modifiers.

1. While dangling feet in the ocean, a dolphin tickled me.

2. Jutting out of the sea, the swimmers were shocked to see a fin.

3. With its head poked in the sand, I noticed the crab's monstrous claws.

4. Riding horseback along the beach, the ocean looked very peaceful.

5. Why did you buy saltwater taffy from a store that was unwrapped?

6. A big wave wiped out the sand castle Joe had built unexpectedly.

7. My mother told me to put on sunscreen at least ten times this week.

8. I repaired the raft that was punctured by the shark with great care.

Name

Copyright © 2014 World Book, Inc./ Incentive Publications, Chicago, IL

TROUBLE IN A BOTTLE

The trouble in each bottle has to do with misplaced modifiers. They contribute to muddled messages. Help clarify the messages before they float away.

Re-write each sentence in the space near the bottle to make its meaning clear.

1. THE SURFER SPOTTED A SHARK IN HER WET SUIT.

2. BRETT AND I HAD SAM FOR A SNACK AT OUR CAMPFIRE.

3. WHILE PADDLING HIS BOARD, THREE DOLPHINS TEASED ALONZO.

4. LYING ON THE RAFT, THE SUN BURNED US BADLY.

5. THE BLUE SWIMMER'S GOGGLES WERE SWEPT AWAY BY A WAVE.

6. SOPHIE DROPPED ON THE SAND THE SANDWICH SHE WAS EATING BY MISTAKE.

7. STANDING ON THE SURFBOARD, THE MONSTER WAVE ROARED BEHIND ME.

8. TIRED FROM A JOG ON THE BEACH, THE ICY LEMONADE CALLED OUT TO ME.

9. THE BOYS SERVED S'MORES TO THEIR FRIENDS OOZING WITH MELTED CHOCOLATE.

Name

LOST IN THE WAVE

This story got caught up in a big wave. (So did something else—you'll have to read to find that out!) Unfortunately, all the commas have been lost, making it hard to read.

Find all the places where commas have been washed away. Use a colored pen or pencil to insert them where they belong.

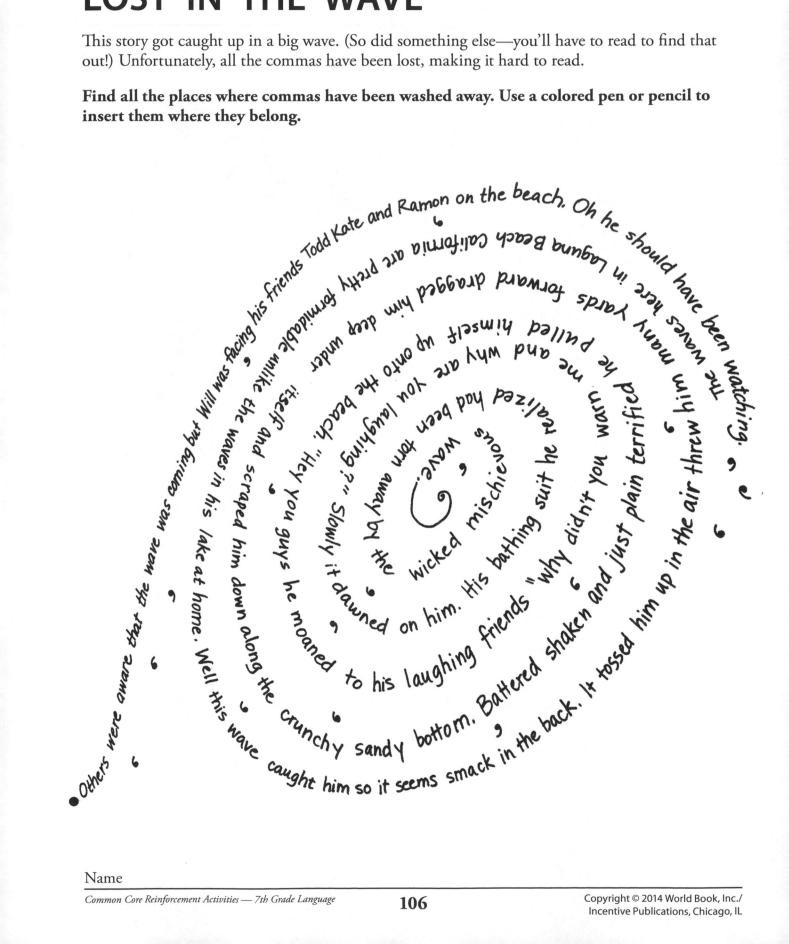

Will was facing his friends Todd, Kate, and Ramon on the beach. Oh, he should have been watching. The waves here in Laguna Beach, California, are pretty formidable, unlike the waves in his lake at home. Well, this wave caught him so, it seems, smack in the back. It tossed him up in the air, threw him many yards forward, dragged him deep under, scraped him down along the crunchy, sandy bottom. Battered, shaken, and just plain terrified, he pulled himself up onto the beach. "Hey, you guys," he moaned to his laughing friends, "why didn't you warn me, and why are you laughing?" Slowly it dawned on him. His bathing suit he realized had been torn away by the wicked, mischievous wave. Others were aware that the wave was coming, but Will was not.

BEACH-BLANKET ERRORS

Some of the signs near this sea town are in need of repair.

Decide which signs contain coordinate adjectives and add commas where needed.

WORDS THAT CONFUSE

I was curtain I would love fishing. Grandfather gave me great advise about witch bait to use, how to make sure the bait is oblivious to the fish, how to cast the line and how to real in the line without loosing the fish. On our first fishing trip, I excepted Grandfather's challenge to a contest. He said he appreciated my positive altitude. In the end, we tied for the number of fish, and though we were tried, Gramps wanted to have a little ceremony before heading home. He gave a speach and officially conducted me into the Willits Family Fishing Club.

This writer, Lewis, is confused, and it's no surprise. Plenty of words in the English language have similar looks, sounds, or meanings. Help him get the right words!

I. Find misspelled or misused words in the story. Write them correctly below.

II. Help Lewis with this spelling assignment. Circle each incorrect word. Write the word that he should have chosen. Spell it correctly.

1. If I could just get trough this week I can get though anything.

2. I wonder weather the whether will get any better.

3. The district attorney decided to persecute the clown for failing to make people laugh.

4. There are allot of buttons to push on the remote control for our new television.

5. I certainly could use a guardian angle today (particularly one who knows geometry).

6. My English teacher says I have a serious lack of comas in my essay.

7. My brother threatened to afflict pain on me if I use his cell phone.

8. I heard you scored 100% on your science test. That's inedible!

Name

Copyright © 2014 World Book, Inc./
Incentive Publications, Chicago, IL

LESSONS LEARNED AT THE BEACH

Watch out for misspellings in this tale about Lola at the beach.

Read each sentence carefully. If there is a misspelled word, cross it out and write it correctly in the blank. If all the words are spelled correctly, write OK in the blank.

I can't wait to try out my new suit!

I'm sure it will be notised!

_____ 1. It was a beautifull day on the beach.

_____ 2. Lola had recieved a new bathing suit for her birthday.

_____ 3. It was a generos gift from her cousin.

_____ 4. She was anxious to try it out in the ocean.

_____ 5. Her friends gave her lots of complements.

_____ 6. "I'm so excited!" she exclamed.

_____ 7. Her urge to jump in the water was uncontrolable.

_____ 8. Could the water have been any more pleasent?

_____ 9. Splashing and leaping, Lola was really enjoying herself.

_____ 10. Unfortunatly, a jellyfish was enjoying itself in the ocean, too.

_____ 11. Thanks to a nasty sting, Lola's adventure ended early.

_____ 12. She was truely sorry she hadn't been more careful.

_____ 13. On her beach trip beach, she will probally look before she swims!

_____ 14. Hopefully, she'll rember to use sunscreen next time, as well.

Correct any misspelled words in Lola's comments by the picture.

Name _____

Copyright © 2014 World Book, Inc./
Incentive Publications, Chicago, IL

Common Core Reinforcement Activities — 7th Grade Language

A WORDY LOVE LETTER

Patch the Pirate has a problem.
He wants to write a beautiful love letter to Mermaid Maryann, but he doesn't know how. He has found a local writer who will put his words on paper, but the writer charges one coin per word and Patch only has forty coins. He needs your help!

Eliminate the excess and imprecise words. Re-write this letter in forty or fewer words. Write it below; there are forty lines to help you keep Patch within his budget (put one word on each line).

> My Dearest Maryann,
>
> You are the most totally amazing mermaid in the whole entire ocean. My heart does a flip-flop whenever you are near and I think you're beautiful. Your sweet, lovely face sparkles in the water and reminds me of twinkling stars in the sky. Will you marry me and be my wife? I would be so completely honored if you would say yes. We could be husband and wife and rule the ocean together as its king and queen. What do you think? Will you consider marrying me?
>
> All My Love Forever and Always for Eternity,
>   Patch

_____ _____ _____ _____ _____

_____ _____ _____ _____ _____

_____ _____ _____ _____ _____

_____ _____ _____ _____ _____

_____ _____ _____ _____ _____

_____ _____ _____ _____ _____

_____ _____ _____ _____ _____

_____ _____ _____ _____ _____

Name

Copyright © 2014 World Book, Inc./
Incentive Publications, Chicago, IL

THE WORDS YOU CHOOSE

Many words have sounds or meanings that are similar to others. The words you choose for a certain situation make all the difference in the meaning of the sentences. Watch what you choose!

Distinguish between the two bold words; then answer the question by circling the correct bold word.

1. These waves are *huge*! Are they **momentous** or **monumental**?

2. Yes, the waters around us are definitely *agitated*. Are they **turbulent** or **tumultuous**?

3. We need to *escape* this situation before disaster strikes. Do we want to **allude** the danger or **elude** it?

4. This storm has *blocked the progress* of our voyage. Has it **stumped** or **stymied** our voyage?

5. Now we find out that this shoreline is a *famous* spot for shipwrecks! Is it a **nefarious** spot or a **notorious** spot?

6. During the last few days, the weather conditions have been *terrible*. Are they **adverse** or **averse**?

7. We were so *gullible* when we believed that the weather is never stormy during August in the South Pacific. Were we **credulous** or **credible**?

8. The crew has been *complaining* constantly. Are they **quarrelsome** or **querulous**?

9. Some sailors are *openly disregarding* their captain's command. Are they **flaunting** or **flouting** his orders?

10. I'll get off this ship any time, but the captain feels *compelled* to stay with his ship. Does he feel **obliged** or **obligated**?

11. This has been the *lowest point* in our ocean adventure. Is it the **nadir** or the **zenith**?

12. I'm going to be *unwilling* to get on another boat anytime soon. Am I **loath** or **loathe** to board another ship?

Name _____

CLUES YOU CAN USE

The sentences about a sandcastle project may contain some unfamiliar words. One strategy to help infer the meaning of a word is to use the context, or the setting, of the word in a sentence.

Find context clues to help you guess the meaning of each word in bold type. Then use your dictionary to compare the actual meaning to your guess.

1. We appreciate your **largesse** in donating all the buckets for our sand castle project.

   Your guess at the meaning:

2. There is a **paucity** of shovels for this job, so we need to find several more.

   Your guess at the meaning:

3. Alex is reluctant to work, so could you gently **cajole** him into helping out?

   Your guess at the meaning:

4. It's Tom's job to keep out any **interlopers** who might come into this area and try to destroy our sand castles.

   Your guess at the meaning:

5. You promised to be on our sand castle building team, and now you are joining another team. How **duplicitous** of you!

   Your guess at the meaning:

6. There will be no **raucous** behavior that might knock down the sand castles!
   Your guess at the meaning:

7. I'll lie on my raft and be rocked to sleep by the gentle **undulation** of the waves.

   Your guess at the meaning:

8. When we're done, fellow beach-goers will show their **adulation** for our amazing creations!

   Your guess at the meaning:

Name

Copyright © 2014 World Book, Inc./
Incentive Publications, Chicago, IL

WHICH WORD?

Choosing exactly the right words can give your sentence a powerful punch. But you have to choose a word that says just what you mean to say.

Which of the bold words is best for the context of each sentence? Use references to find the meanings of the words. Then circle the best choice.

1. We need to (**augment** or **compliment**) this structure because we don't have enough sections in our sandcastle.

2. Our tools are all missing! Someone must have (**absconded** or **gamboled**) with them!

3. The castle must be just right because the judges will (**rectify** or **scrutinize**) every inch of it.

4. Digging up all this wet sand has been a (**tortuous** or **sumptuous**) job.

5. I'm worried about these waves threatening our sandcastles. Maybe the better weather and dying winds will (**quell** or **encourage**) the rough waters.

6. The supply of workers on this project is (**superfluous** or **superior**). We'll need to send some people away.

7. When Abby kicked sand in your eyes, you showed your (**pique** or **tolerance**) by waving your arms and yelling.

8. We became (**reticent** or **cognizant**) of that strange smell when the wind started blowing from the east.

9. The (**acrid** or **acrimonious**) smell convinced us there was a dead animal around somewhere.

10. Zeke headed to the snack bar for six hot dogs to satisfy his (**voracious** or **egregious**) appetite.

Name

WHAT DO YOU MEAN?

When a sentence contains a challenging vocabulary word, try to understand its meaning by looking for clues in the words around it. These sentences might challenge you!

Choose the best meaning for each bold word from the choices below. Write the correct definition letter in the blank. The example is done for you.

A stealthy submarine slinks along on its *clandestine* mission.   I

1. The crab dug a cozy **niche** in the sand.   _____

2. What a **rueful** sound is coming from that poor beached whale!   _____

3. The **skittish** swimmer tests the cold water with one toe.   _____

4. Pirates **loiter** on the beach, seeming to have no purpose.   _____

5. That painful sunburn caused her to become crabby and **irascible**!   _____

6. Once that **garrulous** couple set up next to us, we had no moments of peace.   _____

7. Did you hear the **impromptu** concert given by the vacationing **virtuoso**?   _____ _____

8. The sassy girl on the pier was quite **insolent**.   _____

9. We were **chagrined** when our friend made fun of our surfing.   _____

10. A **patron** of the snack stand mistakenly paid double for his candy.   _____

Shhhh!

A. menacing
B. excessively talkative
C. excellent musician
D. rude, disrespectful
E. spontaneous

F. sad
G. customer
H. short on money
I. secret
J. exotic

K. embarrassed, disappointed
L. cranny
M. nervous, anxious
N. very irritable
O. hang around wasting time

Name

I'M SUBMERSIBLE!

The word *submersible* is made of several parts. To understand the meaning of the whole word, it helps to know the meanings of the root, prefix, and suffix!

Find the right word parts to build a new word that matches each meaning. When you combine the parts, the spelling of the root may change.

1. scene with water _____

2. result of being broken _____

3. roll again _____

4. relating to the end _____

5. work together _____

6. able to be carried across _____

7. area of atmosphere and space _____

8. pertaining to sound _____

9. to put into words _____

10. one who works on the sea _____

11. science of the Earth _____

12. pertaining to athletes _____

13. beneath the sea _____

14. relating to heat _____

15. self writing _____

16. made of wood _____

Name _____

Copyright © 2014 World Book, Inc./
Incentive Publications, Chicago, IL

Common Core Reinforcement Activities — 7th Grade Language

IT'S INCONCEIVABLE!

The word *inconceivable* is formed from the root word *conceive*, the prefix *in-*, and the suffix *–able*. If you understand the meanings of the word parts, this will help you figure out the meaning of the whole word!

Below are the meanings of some common roots. Your task is to make new words by adding one or more prefixes or suffixes (or both) to each root. In the space below each item, write the meaning of the new word.

It is not inconceivable that a predator might be invisible in the murkiness of the ocean!

1. tort (*twist*) _____

2. lum (*light*) _____

3. therm (*heat*) _____

4. vis (*see*) _____

5. tele (*far*) _____

6. rot (*turn*) _____

7. flam (*fire*) _____

8. astr (*star*) _____

9. pop (*people*) _____

10. ped (*foot*) _____

11. loc (*place*) _____

12. culp (*blame*) _____

13. nat (*born*) _____

14. sect (*cut*) _____

15. ann (*year*) _____

16. gyr (*whirl*) _____

Name _____

Copyright © 2014 World Book, Inc./
Incentive Publications, Chicago, IL

WOULD YOU? COULD YOU? SHOULD YOU?

You can't possibly decide how to respond to these curious inquiries unless you know the meanings of all the words in the question! When a word's context does not give a clue to the meaning, consult a dictionary for help.

Find the meaning of each bold word. Then use your understanding of the word to answer the question *yes*, *no*, or *possibly*. Be prepared to defend your choice!

_____ 1. Should you get into an **altercation** with an octopus?

_____ 2. Could you raise **mollusks** in a metropolis?

_____ 3. Should you expect a **scoundrel** to **prevaricate**?

_____ 4. Could you serve shrimp on a **peccadillo**?

_____ 5. Would you eat an **affidavit** with syrup?

_____ 6. Could you play a **piccolo** on a **tombolo**?

_____ 7. Could you wrap a **tarpon** in a **tarpaulin**?

_____ 8. Would you rent a raft from a **charlatan**?

_____ 9. Could you wear a wet suit during a **debacle**?

_____ 10. Could you sing an **archipelago** in an opera?

_____ 11. Would you ride a jet ski with a **gargoyle**?

_____ 12. Would you fill a **bathyscaphe** with bubble bath?

_____ 13. Should you share your lunch with an **omnivore**?

_____ 14. Would you loan your surfboard to a **nonagenarian**?

_____ 15. Would you invite the pope to take part in a **brouhaha**?

_____ 16. Should you decline to board a raft that is not **buoyant**?

_____ 17. Should you be vehement about wearing a lifejacket on a **dinghy**?

_____ 18. Should you choose a **lackadaisical** person to be your diving partner?

Name _____

117

Common Core Reinforcement Activities — 7th Grade Language

WHERE WOULD YOU FIND IT?

Where would you find a vicar, a carbuncle, or a nautilus? If you don't know the meanings of the words, it will be hard to decide! You'll need to consult a dictionary for help.

Find the meaning of each bold word. Circle the place you'd be likely to find it.

1. **armada**   inside a mitten   on a banana split   on a windshield   in the ocean

2. **garnish**   under your skin   in a paint can   on a roast beef   in a tool shed

3. **dendrite**   in a nerve cell   on a cell phone   in an envelope   on a pizza

4. **cochlea**   in a sandwich   in your ear   on a propeller   on a menu

5. **sepal**   in a movie theater   in a milkshake   on a leaf   in a sermon

6. **nebula**   behind a dog's ear   at the dry cleaners   in outer space   in a canal

7. **bibelot**   riding a carousel   climbing a tree   in a diary   on a shelf

8. **tourniquet** making a movie   in a parade   around a leg   on a sundae

9. **corona**   dancing at a wedding around the sun   under a bed   in a purse

10. **vicar**   on a leash   on a baked potato   at a church   in a barrel

11. **carbuncle** on your face   in an auto engine   in a clothes dryer   on a swing

12. **monologue** floating in a creek   in a drama   in a shoebox   in a diaper

13. **nautilus**   making pancakes   swimming in the sea   eating grass   at a pep rally

14. **septum**   in your nose   on your eyebrows   inside a sewer   at a cemetery

15. **pinnacle**   on a cathedral   on a hot dog   on a pin cushion   on a leash

16. **oxymoron**   riding a train   in a speech   in a grotto   in beef stew

17. **lexicon**   on a tire   in a library   at a rock concert   in a canoe

18. **euphonium**

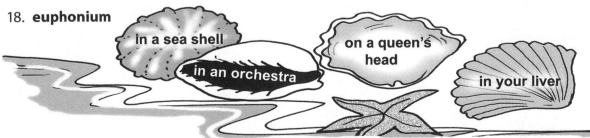

in a sea shell   in an orchestra   on a queen's head   in your liver

Name _____

Copyright © 2014 World Book, Inc./
Incentive Publications, Chicago, IL

TAKE THE GOOD ADVICE

Below are some important words of advice for any beachgoer.
To understand the advice, however, you'll need to know the
meanings of all the words in each sentence.

**Decide the meaning of each bold word. Answer the question.
Consult a dictionary to verify your decision.
Be ready to defend your answers.**

1. Don't get **churlish** around sharks. Why not?

2. Keep your **proboscis** away from all jellyfish. Why?

3. Never water-ski behind a boat with a **dormant** driver. Why not?

4. Don't shake hands with an **anemone**. Why not?

5. Don't wear **jodhpurs** when you go snorkeling. Why not?

6. Don't depend on a lifeguard who has **aquaphobia**. Why not?

7. Swim only where there is a **dearth** of seaweed. Why?

8. Don't **meander** into murky waters with a manta ray. Why not?

9. Avoid signing up for lessons with an **inept** dive instructor. Why?

10. Don't let your boat get caught in a **maelstrom**. Why not?

11. Don't intercede in a **fracas** between two sea lions. Why not?

12. Keep your kayak away from **turbulent** waters. Why?

Name _____

HEAD IN THE CLOUDS

Has anyone every called you a ham? Chances are, they meant you were a show-off or being overly dramatic. In that case, "ham" is an idiom. An idiom is a form of figurative speaking that is not taken literally, but rather has a different established meaning that's unique to a specific language or group.

Choose four idioms from the sentences below or from the illustration. Draw a picture to show what each would mean if the words were taken literally. Do one drawing here and the others on the back of the page. Then for all the examples, write what the idioms really mean.

They thought I was off my rocker when I tried this sport, but now they can eat their hearts out. My head's in the clouds! From now on when it comes to parasailing, the sky's the limit!

1. You've got a bee in your bonnet.

2. He swallowed my story hook, line, and sinker.

3. She's got too many irons in the fire.

4. This information is straight from the horse's mouth.

5. Mom is really in hot water now.

6. I know she has skeletons in her closet.

7. Once again, she put her foot in her mouth.

8. Your goose is cooked.

9. I'll pull some strings to get you a ticket.

10. I went out on a limb for her when she needed help.

Name _____

Copyright © 2014 World Book, Inc./
Incentive Publications, Chicago, IL

DON'T CHICKEN OUT!

"Be a good egg and go first," my friends begged as they urged me to try parasailing. The idea of being up that high sailing behind a boat blew my mind, but I decided to bite the bullet and go for it. When it was time to sign the papers, I got cold feet and almost backed out. But Julie said, "You're not chickening out, are you, Al?" Now I was really under the gun. I was sweating bullets—even with the ocean breeze. I needed to get this group off my back, so I paid my money. I was shaking in my boots when I stepped onto the boat. With my heart in my throat, I buckled the harness, and the wind began to lift me up. Before long, I was soaring high, feeling like a million bucks, and having more fun than a barrel of monkeys!

Figurative language uses words in unusual ways. Instead of giving precise meaning, the words create an image that communicates meaning with fun and flair. As you can see, there are no actual chickens in this story.

Circle the examples of figurative language in the parasailing speaker's tale. Then use at least six figures of speech in your own short paragraph or story.

A few ideas:
• *a bone to pick with you*
• *bats in her belfry*
• *bring home the bacon*
• *cry your eyes out*
• *by the skin of your teeth*
• *in the doghouse*
• *face the music*
• *jump the gun*
• *lose your head*
• *heart on your sleeve*
• *raining cats and dogs*
• *behind the eight ball*
• *on the money*
• *just under the wire*
• *in the nick of time*
• *right up my alley*
• *that takes the cake*
• *stick your neck out*

Name _____

SEASIDE ANALOGIES

The fate of a swimmer may be related to the speed of this lifeguard. Here's an activity about another kind of relationship. An **analogy** shows a relationship between two sets of words. The relationship between the first two words is the same as the relationship between the second set of words.

A. Lifeguard is to **rescue** AS **attorney** is to **defend.**

(*The second word in each pair shows the job or action of the first word.*)

B. Jovial is to **solemn** AS **punctual** is to **tardy.**

(*The words in each pair are antonyms.*)

C. Deliberate is to **contemplate** AS **foster** is to **encourage.**

(*The words in each pair are synonyms.*)

Here's a challenging exercise to do at the beach . . . or anywhere else. Find a word on one of the life preservers that completes each analogy.

1. Mesmerize *is to* _____ AS curtail *is to* shorten.

2. _____ *is to* inept AS opulence *is to* opulent.

3. Lyrics *is to* poet AS _____ *is to* journalist.

4. Trachea *is to* _____ AS stomach *is to* digestion.

5. Amicable *is to* friendly AS languid *is to* _____ .

6. Tornado *is to* chaos AS lullaby *is to* _____ .

7. _____ *is to* poison AS verbiage is *to* words.

8. Candidate *is to* campaign AS _____ *is to* investigation.

9. Appetizer *is to* canapé AS _____ *is to* borscht.

10. Hoodwink *is to* _____ AS preach *is to* parson.

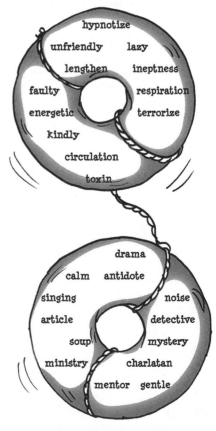

hypnotize
unfriendly   lazy
lengthen   ineptness
faulty   respiration
energetic   terrorize
kindly
circulation
toxin

drama
calm   antidote
singing   noise
article   detective
soup   mystery
ministry   charlatan
mentor   gentle

Name _____

Copyright © 2014 World Book, Inc./ Incentive Publications, Chicago, IL

CURIOUS RELATIONSHIPS

In an analogy, the first pair of words must have the same relationship as the words in the second pair. When you try to solve an analogy, begin by deciding what the relationship is between the two words you are given. There are several different kinds of relationships found in analogies. In the analogy below, *pinch* is a function or action of a *crab*. Fill in the blank with a word that names something whose function is to *cut*.

Crab: pinch :: _____ : cut.

Decide what the word relationship is for each analogy. Write the code letter at the beginning of each example (see the box). Then circle the word that best completes the analogy.

_____ 1. Repose : rest :: : vacillate

    roam   waiver   certify   relax

_____ 2. Peril : perilous :: _____ : conductivity

    conduct   conductor   electronics   activity

_____ 3. _____ : ladder :: drop : anchor

    sailor   rungs   climb   carry

_____ 4. Flurries : _____ :: sprinkles : downpour

    snow   weather   sleet   blizzard

_____ 5. Hammer : pound :: shower : _____

    water   tub   cleanse   build

_____ 6. Channel : buoy :: _____ : aria

    opera   ocean   airport   cavern

_____ 7. Disapprove : condone :: avarice : _____

    approve   generosity   greed   average

_____ 8. _____ : beverage :: cannelloni : food

    liquid   cappuccino   pasta   carafe

Codes
S = synonym
A = antonym
C = in the same category
D = degree
F = function
L = location
W = word form
R = response or action

Name _____

Common Core Reinforcement Activities — 7th Grade Language

BENEATH THE SURFACE

The **denotation** (dictionary definition) of *treasure* is "wealth stored up or hoarded."

But beneath the surface, there is more to a word than its strict definition. The word *treasure* also stirs up all kinds of images and ideas of buried treasure chests, gold and silver, pirates, pirate ships, deserted islands, maps, picks and shovels, adventure, and great riches. All these and other images suggested by the word *treasure* make up its **connotation**.

Find the *denotation* of each word. Then write another word or phrase with a similar denotation that conveys a *connotation* fitting to the picture.

1. marooned _____

_____

2. shark _____

_____

3. hungry _____

_____

4. discouraged _____

_____

5. alone _____

_____

Name

124

Copyright © 2014 World Book, Inc./
Incentive Publications, Chicago, IL

CHOOSE CAREFULLY

The survivors were uneasy when they saw the shark fins circling.

Notice how the sentence feels different when it begins in one of these ways:

> The survivors were terrified when they saw . . .
>
> The survivors felt desperate when they saw . . .
>
> The survivors were panicked when they saw . . .

Uneasy, terrified, desperate, and *panicked* have similar meanings, but the connotation of *uneasy* does not have the strong fear component. Even when words have similar denotations, their connotations can give entirely different impressions. So choose your words carefully; word choice makes a difference in the impact and meaning!

Explain how the connotation of the word in the second sentence changes the sentence meaning.

1. The shark was **mad** when we kicked at him.

   The shark became **enraged** when we kicked at him.

2. A **rainstorm** swept across the island.

   A **hurricane** swept across the island.

3. The others **criticized** my attempts to start a fire.

   The others **ridiculed** my attempts to start a fire.

4. That **troublesome** monkey has annoyed us all day.

   That **infuriating** monkey has annoyed us all day.

5. The tropical sun **burned** our fair skin.

   The tropical sun **scorched** our fair skin.

Name

THE LANGUAGE OF TIDES

To talk about tides, you need to know the language! Any content area you study—in any subject—will have its own unique vocabulary. In order to learn new content, you will need to be able to recognize and use these new words.

Read the article as it is. Then, use a dictionary to find the definitions of the bold words. Write them below. Next, read the article again and refer to your definitions when needed. Finally, draw a diagram on a separate piece of paper that shows something you learned from this article. Label the diagram.

*Tide is a **periodic** motion of water in the oceans. Tides result primarily from variations in the **gravitational pull** of the moon and sun on different parts of Earth. Tides cause the water level at any place in the oceans to rise and fall in **cycles**. In a typical cycle, the water level gradually rises to **high tide**, then falls. After reaching **low tide**, the water level starts to rise again. During a tidal cycle, **tidal currents** also reverse direction. In coastal areas, tidal changes in water level are larger and tidal currents are stronger compared to those in the open ocean.*

periodic:

gravitational pull:

cycles:

high tide:

low tide:

tidal currents:

Name

Copyright © 2014 World Book, Inc./
Incentive Publications, Chicago, IL

ASSESSMENT AND ANSWER KEYS

ENGLISH LANGUAGE ARTS ASSESSMENT

PART ONE: READING

The Rubber-Band Man

Stretch McCoy is the greatest bungee jumper alive. His legs are so elastic that he does not need the usual bungee cord for the sport. He has defied death hundreds of times. Beyond that, his speed and strength astonish all onlookers.

Once, he leapt from the top of Mt. Everest, dropping all the way to the base of the mountain where he scooped up a can of snow, mixed it with cola, and guzzled it down before being snapped back up to the mountain top. Another time, Stretch jumped from a bridge in the Amazon, hurtling straight down into the mouth of a crocodile. He bounced up and down five times—in and out of the croc's jaws. On the last trip down, he wrestled the crocodile in a move as swift as a sneeze and left the baffled beast exhausted on the riverbank.

Stretch has been known to bungee jump while hula hooping, while barbequing a steak, and while playing a piano. His ability to carry that hoop, grill, or piano right along with him stuns his fans. You can **surmise** how strong he is. He is so strong that . . . well, now, that's another story, isn't it?

1. Describe the narrator's viewpoint about Mr. McCoy.

2. What is the central idea that affects all the events in the text?

3. Circle at least four phrases or sentences that support the claim of the opening sentence.

4. What can you infer about Mr. McCoy that is not directly stated?

5. What does the author accomplish with the phrase ***in a move as swift as a sneeze*** (paragraph 2)?

6. What is the meaning of ***surmise*** in paragraph 3?

Name

7. What is the theme of the poem?

8. What details are used to support the theme?

The travel bug **beckons**

Lures to **locales** exotic and far—

Places with mysteries unveiled.

New sights, new **plights**, new promises,

All calling your name, calling your name.

But travelers beware; visitors take care,

Dangers, discomforts, distresses are there.

Alaska's cold will grab your throat.

The Sahara will choke you with tight thirst.

Death Valley—just the name says, "Don't!"

The Amazon will send slimy, hissing serpents

To slither alongside your boat.

9. Underline examples of rhyme and alliteration. What do these word choice devices add to the effect of the poem?

10. Circle examples of personification. How do these strengthen the author's message?

11. What purpose is served by the repetition in line 5?

What is the meaning of these words in the poem?

12. **beckons** _____

13. **locales** _____

14. **plights** _____

Name _____

10 Steps to Build a Fire

You'll need to know how to build a fire if you want to warm yourself up on a chilly camping trip, signal for help in case you get lost, cook some hot food outdoors, or dry out a damp sleeping bag. Here's how to do it.

Step 1: On all outings, carry matches and some paper or cardboard for starting a fire. Keep your matches in a plastic bag so they stay dry,

Step 2: On site, gather fuel for burning. You will need tinder (something thin and dry like leaves or bark or wood you shave with your knife), kindling (small dry sticks or dead branches), and larger pieces of dry wood to keep your fire going longer.

Step 3: Choose a flat site for the fire—one that is away from trees, grass, or bushes that could catch fire. Look for a spot that is protected from the wind.

Step 4: Dig a shallow fire pit in the ground. Build a ring of rocks around it to keep sparks and embers contained.

Step 5: Get a supply of water. Keep this nearby.

Step 6: Pile some tinder loosely in the center of the pit.

Step 7: Arrange the kindling in a teepee style, leaning the tops of the sticks together over the kindling.

Step 8: Light the tinder in a few different places. If the fire has trouble igniting, blow gently on it.

Step 9: When you have a crackling fire and the teepee collapses, lay bigger pieces of wood criss-cross right over the hottest part of the fire.

Step 10: Never leave your fire unattended. Make sure your fire is completely out before you leave. Pour water over it if necessary. The coals should be cool enough to touch. Check it twice.

15. What is the purpose of the text?

16. How does the writing style and structure help the author accomplish the purpose?

17. What can you infer about the topic that is not directly stated?

18. Write a two- or three-sentence summary of the text.

Name

Copyright © 2014 World Book, Inc./
Incentive Publications, Chicago, IL

Shake, rattle and roll at the **No Boundaries Cafe.**

Convergent boundaries are boundaries between two colliding plates. When two oceanic plates collide (or one oceanic and one continental), one is forced down. The area where the plate submerges is the *subduction zone.* When two continental plates collide, the rocks crumble and rise, forming folded mountains.

Divergent boundaries are boundaries where two plates pull apart.

Transform faults are boundaries where plates slide or scrape past each other. These are often areas of earthquake activity!

I think I'll order the blue plate special.

Identify three main ideas from the text.
Explain how the author uses the visual presentation to strengthen each idea.

	Main Ideas	How the Illustration Reinforces the Idea
19.		
20.		
21.		

Name

Copyright © 2014 World Book, Inc./
Incentive Publications, Chicago, IL

———— Leave Pythons in the Wild ————

Do you long for a pet but have allergies to all things furry or hairy? Do you want to impress your friends by having the coolest pet of all? Do you think it would be comforting to have a smooth, silky friend around your shoulders at all times? Do you think snakes are easier to care for than other pets? Whatever your reason for wanting a python—I urge you: Do not get one.

Pythons are high maintenance. I speak as a former python owner. I had to clean the aquarium often and check every day to be sure a fungus was not growing in the shavings. Pythons need a precise temperature during the day and a different one at night, so we were constantly monitoring the temperature. She drank so much water that I had to check the dish several times a day. Sometimes she wouldn't eat, and I had to force-feed her. Other times she threw up her food. Believe me, cleaning up a half-digested rat is no fun!

My friends were impressed for a while, but they soon went on to the next cool thing. Anyway, I learned that walking around with the snake a lot was not healthy for her. Priscilla started off as a cute little thing, but grew to a 25-foot long, 150-pound giant. It became hard to pick her up, uncomfortable to carry her, and difficult to provide enough room for her. It quickly became less fun.

Also, it was not much fun to handle the mice or small rats to feed the snake. It was not fun to soak her when she was shedding her skin. And I had to put up with some nasty bites that got infected.

It's expensive to own a python; we were constantly buying live food, and the vet that specialized in snakes was 50 miles away and charged high fees. Like most pythons, Priscilla escaped all the time. On one occasion, she hid out in the neighbor's yard and killed their cat. That was a great loss for them and another expense for our family!

My most urgent warning to you about pythons is this: they pose a danger to small children. Pythons wrap themselves around small creatures and suffocate them—and an unsupervised child mixed with an escapist python can turn deadly.

Owning a python is not worth the dangers, risks, work, and cost. And even then, with a snake that is so good at escaping any enclosure, the dangers to small children and animals are not worth the risk of any joys you might find in being a snake owner. Find another way to be cool. Find a pet that is easier and friendlier.

22. What is the author's claim?

23. Underline evidence the author used to support her key claim. Did she use sound reasoning and strong evidence?

24. Are you convinced of her position? Tell why or why not.

Name

132

Copyright © 2014 World Book, Inc./
Incentive Publications, Chicago, IL

PART TWO: WRITING

1. Think about places you would rather NOT go or do on an adventure. Choose one of the ideas below, or start with an idea of your own. Write a clear, convincing argument in favor of your opinion. Add supporting details. Include a dynamic opening and summarizing conclusion.

_____

_____

_____

_____

_____

_____

_____

_____

_____

_____

_____

_____

_____

_____

a sinking ship

center of a hurricane

bottom of a crevasse

bee-keeping school

zoo with broken cages

principal's office

spinach-eating contest

chasing desert mirages

garbage sorting

Name

Copyright © 2014 World Book, Inc./
Incentive Publications, Chicago, IL

Common Core Reinforcement Activities — 7h Grade Language

2. In ten steps or fewer, explain how to keep a friendship.
Include an opening and closing statement.

I always give
my friend the best
presents!

_____

_____

_____

_____

_____

_____

_____

2. Write an anecdote (short story) about your most embarrassing moment. It can be real or
fictitious. Start with a catchy beginning that sets the stage (where, when, who); give details
about what happened, and wrap up with a strong ending.

Name

PART THREE: LANGUAGE A—Conventions

Describe the function of the bolded phrase in the sentence.

1. Eager surfers welcomed **waves rising like walls**.

2. **Encountering a shark** is quite an experience!

Describe the function of the bolded clause in the sentence.

3. **Because Tad had waited the longest,** I let him catch the wave.

4. Lolly is the diver **who owns the red mask**.

5. She screamed **as if a shark was following her**.

Rewrite each sentence to straighten out the misplaced modifiers.

6. After falling off the surfboard, the shark circled me three times.

7. The pink surfer's wetsuit was washed away by a wave.

Insert any missing commas in each sentence.

8. We expected a long cold wait for some good waves.

9. Shall we avoid that littered seaweed-strewn part of the beach?

10. Meg ended up with multiple jellyfish stings.

Name

Read the passage below. Circle any misspelled words. Write them correctly on the lines.

How to Avoid a Shark Attack

1. Increase your knowlege about sharks.

2. Be watchfull at all times.

3. Don't venchure into the water alone.

4. Stay away from shark-invested waters.

5. Keep the boat or shore in site. Have an excape plan.

6. Carry a spear gun. It can be your best allie.

7. Avoid wearing bright colours or flashy jewlry.

8. Swim gently. Don't thrash arms or legs in a frensy.

9. Stay out of the water if you are bleeding.

10. Don't ever distrub or provoke a shark.

11. _____

12. _____

13. _____

14. _____

15. _____

16. _____

17. _____

18. _____

19. _____

20. _____

In each example, circle the word choice that is spelled correctly for the context.

21. Did you manage to (**elude, allude**) the shark out by the reef?

22. After his encounter with the barracuda, Julian is (**adverse, averse**) to snorkeling.

23. The water is so choppy that I'm (**loathe, loath**) to get in right now.

24. Angelina could not think of anything to do (**except, accept**) to swim for the boat.

25. You can bet we all did a (**through, thorough, though**) reading of the shark-safety manual after that last diving trip!

Name _____

Copyright © 2014 World Book, Inc./
Incentive Publications, Chicago, IL

PART FOUR: LANGUAGE B—Vocabulary

Add prefixes and/or suffixes to form a word from each root. Write the meaning for each word you create.

1. fer

_____

2. therm

_____

3. tele

_____

4. graph

_____

5. ject

_____

6. scend

_____

7. dorm

_____

Use context clues to guess at the meaning of the bold word in each statement. Write your guess near the speech balloon.

8 Before heading to the beach, I read that news story in the Village Morning **Gazette** about the beached whale.

I intended to kayak all day, but my plans were **foiled** by the stormy weather. 9

10 There goes show-off Lexie down the beach wildly **brandishing** that expensive new boogey board.

After reports of shark attacks, the fearful surfers approach the water with **trepidation**. 11

12 The sky was clear a few minutes ago! Those clouds seem to have **materialized** out of nowhere!

Name

Copyright © 2014 World Book, Inc./
Incentive Publications, Chicago, IL

Common Core Reinforcement Activities — 7h Grade Language

Describe the relationship between the two bold words in each sentence.

13. How long did that **dispute** last? They seemed to **squabble** for hours.

14. It must be a nightmare for an **octopod** to try to **pedal** a bike!

15. **Energetic** Emily swims circles around **lethargic** Lacy.

Circle the word that best finishes the analogy. Write a word to describe the relationships between the pairs of words.

16. **Peril :** _____ **:: hectic : chaotic**

turmoil   peace   danger   purpose

_____

17. **Attorney :** courtroom **::** _____ **: train**

lawsuit   conductor   engine   caboose

_____

18. _____ **: hilarious :: serious : critical**

amusing   tragic   astonishing   awful

_____

19. **Spaghetti :** _____ **:: cedar : evergreen**

Italian   stringy   hungry   pasta

_____

20. **Novice : pro :: midnight :** _____

dark   night   treachery   noon

_____

Write a meaning for each bold expression.

21. Marianna thought she **had that ski race in the bag!**

22. After losing the race, she proclaimed, "You haven't seen the last of me yet. **There's more than one way to skin a cat!**"

Circle the best word choice.

23. Exhausted and battered from fighting the surf, Georgio _____ down the beach.

meandered   staggered

scampered   walked

24. Look at the _____ fireworks splattering the sky over the beach.

elegant   graceful

spectacular   handsome

Name _____

Copyright © 2014 World Book, Inc./
Incentive Publications, Chicago, IL

ASSESSMENT ANSWER KEY

Part One: Reading

1. Narrator is in awe of McCoy.
2. McCoy's extremely stretchy legs
3. Answers will vary. There are many possibilities.
4. Possible answers: He is a risk-taker; he loves danger and adventure; he is somewhat of a show-off
5. Possible answers: amuses the reader; creatively shows the speed of the crocodile wrestling; gives a concrete and common example of speediness to the winner.
6. guess
7. Answers may vary; caution
8. *travelers beware, visitors take care; Dangers, discomforts, distresses are there;* or any of the last 5 lines
9. rhyme: *beware, care, there; sights, plights;* alliteration: *Dangers, discomforts, distresses; slimy hissing serpents, slither*
10. *Alaska's cold will grab your throat; The Sahara will choke you with tight thirst;* answers to the question will vary.
11. repetition: Answers will vary.
12. calls
13. places
14. predicaments
15. to explain how to build a fire
16. Answers will vary;

possibly: the steps make the explanation clear and give the reader small portions to "digest" one at a time. The style is straightforward and simple which keeps the message uncluttered by excess words.
17. Answers will vary; possibly: One must pay attention to safety when dealing with fire building.
18. Check summaries for coverage of main points, use of their own words, coherence, completeness, and conciseness.
19. - 21. At divergent boundaries, plates in Earth's crust collide, resulting in a sinking plate or rocks rising into mountains. (The illustration on left shows plates pushing up a "mountain." At divergent boundaries, plates separate and move apart. (The illustration in center shows two plates far apart.) Plates sliding past each other form transform faults. (The illustration on the right shows plates sliding past each other.)
22. Pythons should not be kept as pets.
23. Look for several underlined phrases or sentences to show evidence used by author. Student opinions will vary as to whether the

reasoning and evidence was strong.
24. Answers will vary.

Part Two: Writing

1 through 3: Student writing will differ. Check all passages to see that they are clear and flow smoothly—and that they follow the directions adequately.

Part Three: Language A– Conventions

1. used as subject of the sentence
2. used as direct object of the verb *welcomed*
3. modifies the verb *let* (tells why)
4. modifies the noun *diver* (tells which diver)
5. modifies the verb *screamed* (tells how)
6. Possible: After I fell off the surfboard, the shark circled me three times.
7. The surfer's pink wetsuit was washed away by a wave.
8. insert comma after *long*
9. insert comma after *littered*
10. no comma needed
11. - 20. knowledge, watchful, venture, infested, escape, ally, colors, jewelry, frenzy, disturb
21. elude
22. averse
23. loath
24. except
25. thorough

Part Four: Language B– Vocabulary

1. - 7. Check to see that students have written words that include each root and that the meanings are reasonable.
8. - 12. Student guesses will vary. Some possibilities are:
8. newspaper
9. stopped; prevented the success of
10. shaking threateningly
11. trembling
12. suddenly appeared
13. synonyms
14. have the same root (*ped*)
15. antonyms
16. danger; words are synonyms
17. conductor; second word shows location where first can be found
18. amusing; second word is greater degree of the first
19. pasta; first words are category, second words are members of the category
20. noon; words are opposites
21. would win the race
22. There are many ways to accomplish something.
23. staggered
24. spectacular

ACTIVITIES ANSWER KEY

Note: There are many cases in which answers may and should vary. Accept an answer if the student can give a reasonable justification with details or reasons to support it.

Reading: Literature (pages 22-42)

page 22

Possible answers:

1. A murder has taken place in an attic. The villain was not held accountable. A sleuth and a coroner found human blood and a body with only three legs intact.
2. The mutilated body was not human. The deceased originally had more than three legs.
3. The dead creature was probably a mosquito; *the blood was human, only three legs were left intact.*
4. Going up the staircase, finding blood, finding a dead body—led the reader to anticipate a resolution, but the phrase *the villain had never paid his debt* left a question as to whether the villain would be found.
5. Answers will vary.

page 23

1. the moon; *watched generations, my nightly rotations, my nightly passage*
2. Answers will vary.
3. environmental change with more human development infringing on natural habitats; *change in the landscape; abundance of wildlife is shrinking; villages and towns have sprawled; electric lights multiply; her nightly food forays are longer; she is still*

hungry at dawn; lights creep closer and closer to her domain
4. that the cats will become extinct; *Will they stop in time? fragile hope; without these glimpses of her beauty*
5. *change, shrinking, sprawled, chaotic, nervously, human intruders, hungry, cities are large enough, fragile hope*

page 24

1. Answers will vary. The emphasis on the truth of the story might show the tone to be urgent, serious, or insistent
2. In the last sentence of the first paragraph, he mentions the folklore and traditions about mermaids.
3. *a large, glistening fish; long, flowing red hair; slim female form of a slender back blending into the shimmering tail; There was no mistake. We all saw her.*
4. Answers will vary.

page 25

Theme is humor (or mystery, justice, accusation, resolution); look for student evidence to justify chosen theme. Summaries will vary; look for indication that student has identified main ideas.

pages 26-27

Check student organizers to see that theme has been identified and character traits have been identified along with adequate substantiating evidence.

page 28

Check summaries for coverage of main points, use of their own words, coherence, completeness, and conciseness.

page 29

1. In Locker #18
2. Matt
   (Locker #16 Tina, pizza; #17 Andrew, Chinese food; #18 Matt, ram; #19 Julio, rat; #20 Meghan, snowball)

pages 30-31

1. The men are from Indostan (India), but the setting is not clear—possibly in India somewhere near an elephant!
2. Main characters are the six blind men and the elephant
3. Each blind man touched a different part of the elephant; the shape and texture of each part gave each man a clue to what the item might be; each man had a different idea; each was partly right but wrong about the whole. Nevertheless, each thought he was right because he did not listen to the others or could not incorporate the others' views.
4. The men disagreed about what the "thing" was.
5. Because they couldn't see, and because they each touched a different part, their "observations" about the elephant were all different. As each revealed

an observation and opinion, the plot of the story built to give a broad picture of the elephant and bring the parts together. This showed that, while each man had an accurate observation, each missed the observation of the whole animal.
6. Answers will vary. Check student organizers to see that theme has been identified and character descriptions have been identified in connection with the theme.

page 32

Guesses at meanings will vary. Definitions are:
interminable-endless
incite-stir up
mayhem chaos
zaniest-most unconventional
materialized-showed up
fracas-noisy disturbance
ecstatic-overjoyed
peculiar-odd, unusual
anomaly-oddity
quirky-strange
surges-sudden powerful movement
myriad-a great number
ineffectual-not producing the desired effect

page 33

Guesses at meanings will vary. Definitions are:
paucity-scarcity
impertinent-rude
divulge-reveal
immune-resistant
confounded-confused
dearth-lack
eclectic-wide-ranging

page 34

Guesses at meanings will vary. Definitions are:
larcenist-thief
ingests-eats or drinks
cater-provide what is needed
centenarian-someone who is 100 years old or older
simultaneously-at exactly the same time
voyagers-travelers
bequeaths-leaves something to someone in a will
cyclone-tropical storm
perish-die
impersonates-imitates
toxic-poisonous
gullet-esophagus
cache-stockpile

page 35

1. Frost poem: aaba; Slone poem: ab, cb, db, eb
2. Answers will vary.
3. Frost poem: see *me stopping, sound's the sweep;* Sloan poem: *When you wish, Keep your kisses*
4. Frost poem: final two lines; Sloan poem: *Keep our promise, Keep your kisses*
5. Answers will vary.

page 36

1. four 2-line stanzas, one 4-line stanza, four 2-line stanzas;
2. lines beginning differently: Green is…, It's the, Green…., You are green when…, or green at the end of a line
3.-4. Answers will vary.
5. metaphor, simile, personification, rhyme, repetition,

Copyright © 2014 World Book, Inc./ Incentive Publications, Chicago, IL

alliteration; examples will vary

page 37

1. Descriptions will vary. Students might point out that the structure visually looks like layers.

2. People are multi-layered and complicated, but the "layers" are interesting and it is worthwhile to take the time to peel away the layers and get to know the layers of a person even if there is some unpleasantness uncovered!

3. perhaps to give the impression of layers

4. She compares herself to layers, to the fragility, to the strength in the many layers, to layers that can be peeled away, to the strong taste and scent, to something that "pushes" people away, to a distinctness, to something flavorful.

5. Words and phrases that are repeated: like the onion; peeling, closer; answers about the effects of repetition will vary.

page 38

Answers about point of view and evidence from text will vary. Students may identify viewpoint of woodcutter (Mr. Axle, the grandmother (Ms. Hood), and the agencies issuing complaint against Mr. Axle.

page 39

1. Todd heard the voice and was inclined to trust the camel. Tara, not hearing the voice, was skeptical about getting on the camel.

2. The narrator seemed to be wary of the old woman and her advice (calling her foolish). The narrator saw their choice as risky, saw Todd as desperate, and described the choice to trust the camel as grasping at a feeble bit of hope.

3. The narrator changed viewpoint, describing the sigh of relief and admitting that the choice led to rescue. But the change still appeared reluctant by the use of risky choice and by reminding the reader that the choice could have led to disaster.

pages 40-41

1.-2. Answers will vary.

page 42

1. - 4. As students will choose varying stories, the answers will vary. Check to see that the table has been filled in completely, and that questions are answered completely.

Reading: Informational Text (pages 44-64)

page 44

Answers will vary.

1. Red pen—*wove a tale, created by Poseidon, god of the sea, Half-human and half-god creatures, The gods punished Atlantis, Plato mixed fable and fact, inhabited by sea creatures such as mermaids and mermen*

2. Blue pen—*Santorini in the Aegean Sea was mostly destroyed by a volcanic eruption, Minoans inexplicably disappeared at*

about the same time, geographical data reveals islands that match Plato's description of Atlantis

page 45

Answers will vary. Look for student citation of evidence to support their inferences. Possible inferences: Caves are dark. Caving is dangerous. It is cold and wet in caves. The ground in caves is uneven or rough. Cave roofs are low. It is very dark in caves. It is easy to get lost in a cave. Caves are deep.

pages 46-47

Answers will vary. Main ideas might be: A pipeline rupture resulted in a large spill of molasses in Honolulu Harbor. The molasses spill caused significant damage and danger to wildlife (and humans) immediately and will continue to do so for a long time. It is not possible to clean up the mess.
Check student graphic organizers for evidence to support each main idea and for an adequate, accurate summary.

page 48

Answers will vary. Main ideas might be: Hundreds of thousands of workers around the world do jobs that contribute to the making and selling of pencils. Without business cooperation and coordination enabled by the free market system, such a product as a pencil might not be possible at an affordable price. Check to see that students have identified evidence to support each main point.

page 49

Summaries will vary. Samples:
A. World records about distances lead one to

conclude that it is harder to walk on your hands than to walk on water.
B. Some couples set love and marriage-related records to celebrate Valentine's Day.
C. Many records are set for movement, strength, and skill but many people set records for inactive feats, as well.
D. Several Guinness World Records involve feats that use the human chin.
E. The Guinness World Records organization publishes guidelines to follow if you want to attempt to set or break a word record.

page 50

1. At the beginning the interviewer does not seem to know what ACW is and thinks that climbing real rocks is preferable. (Evidence: the interviewer's first and third questions)

2. The climber gives several reasons to try ACW climbing and tells the interviewer how fun, safe, and accessible ACW climbing is. (Evidence: Climber answers to questions 3, 4, and 5)

3. By the end, the interviewer seems more open to trying ACW climbing. (Evidence: Interviewer's final statement)

page 51

1. that the chance of getting red is connected to the relationship between the total number of gumballs in the machine and the number of red gumballs.

2. Charlie uses the information given

to him by the storeowner and his understanding of probability to find that his chance of getting red is 1 in 4. He thinks this is a good chance, so he decides that spending his last quarter is worth the risk.

page 52

Guesses at meanings will vary. Definitions are:
fiber-thread
consultant-expert adviser
innovation-new idea or product
reinforcing-strengthening
extraordinary-exceptional
commercial-business, intended to make a profit
casualties-persons injured or killed

page 53

Synonyms will vary. Some possibilities are:
scarab-sacred beetle
amulet-charm
dehydrate-dry
cavity-hole
aromatic-fragrant
adorned-decorated
sacred-revered
sarcophagus-coffer

page 54

Answers will vary. Some possibilities are:

1. *unsinkable; floating luxury hotel; grand palace; huge rooms; gold-plated light fixtures; swimming pool; steam baths; colossal; opulent; disaster struck; her starboard side struck the berg; tearing open five compartments; command went out; sent out distress signals; she sank fast; passengers and crewmembers perished; The sinking of the Titanic was followed by fury*

2. *Despite several warnings; regrettably;*

the company that built the ship had sent only enough lifeboats for half the people on board; carelessness of the pilot

3. *opulent; despite several warnings; regrettably; in their arrogance; not only was the ship sinkable—she sank fast; fury; carelessness; unequal treatment*

page 55
Answers will vary. Look for student evidence and explanation of their answers.

1. people who love adventure and risk or who would like to be more daring
2. exciting, dangerous, risky, inviting, urging (hard sell)
3. Feel the physical thrill of danger.
4. This line contributes to a tone of urging or selling the adventures.

page 56
Possible answers are:

1. by listing expected records for long-distance journeys, followed by a list of unexpected long-distant journeys, ending with one especially outrageous example
2. the namings of the different kinds of journeys
3. The lists of journey after journey, each one seemingly more unusual than the one before it, accumulates to a powerful barrage of fun journeys. This strengthens the author's initial main-idea statement about *so many possibilities!*

page 57
1. Possible answers are: It's visually

interesting. It draws focus to each individual invention. It makes reading easier than getting through long paragraphs. Readers can choose which portions to read.
2. Answers will vary.
3. Answers will vary. Look for adequate explanations of choices.

pages 58-59
Table: Row 1: Check student work for summaries that capture the main point or purpose.
Row 2: Check word choices to see that they do indicate the author's position.
Rows 3 and 4: Answers will vary.
Question: Check student answers for reasonable explanations with citations from the text.

pages 60-61
Answers will vary. Thesis might be: Scuba diving is dangerous.
Main Points might be: Though diving is thrilling, the hazards are not worth the thrills. Air pressure differences and changes, along with use of compressed air, can cause serious or even deadly injuries to the body. Accidents, equipment problems, and sea creatures pose other serious dangers.
Details chosen will vary.
Author's conclusion: Scuba diving is the most dangerous sport.

pages 62-63
1. *large ape-like creature that supposedly lives in the high Himalayan Mountains; tall, upright primate-like, long-haired creature; large footprints; strange calls*
2. Possible answers are:

tales from natives; guides describing footprints; explorers searching for the Yeti; British climbers photographed large footprints on Mt. Everest; climbers reporting sightings and strange calls; 1954 expedition that found an ape-like hair; Italian climber claiming to have seen the Yeti in 1997
3. that it must exist
4. This adds the idea that the Yeti has a human-like face, long arms, and thick legs. It tells that the Yeti is reported to attack villagers. It also gives information about the meaning of the name *Yeti*. It tells a bit more about expeditions to search for the snowman, and gives an explanation for the tracks and the size of the tracks.
5. Reports from remote parts of Asia; sightings reported by Western travelers; footprint photographs from Eric Shipton
6. that no creatures have been captured or seen in several expeditions; that footprints may have been made by bears or other animals and enlarged by melting snow

page 64
Answers to all the questions will vary. Check answers for indication that the student watched and read the speech, identified the main message, gave some responses to both versions of the speech and identified different impact, and used

evidence from the text to support answers.

Writing (pages 66-84)

pages 66-67-68
Plans and writing will vary. On page 67, check to see that student has answered all the questions, identified evidence for each reason, and written a strong concluding statement. On page 68, check argumentative writing for indications of meeting the standards W.7.1a-e.

page 69-70-71
Plans and writing will vary. On page 70, check to see that student has completed all parts of the plan adequately and written a strong concluding statement. On page 71, check explanatory writing for indications of meeting the standards W.7.2a-f.

page 72-73-74
Plans and writing will vary. On page 73, check to see that student has completed all parts of the plan adequately and written a strong concluding statement. On page 74, check explanatory writing for indications of meeting the standards W.7.3a-e.

page 75
1. putrid
2. Slimy
3. curdled
Check word choices and writing for words with strong sensory appeal.

pages 76-77
Paragraphs will vary. Check student paragraphs for flow, varying sentence length, and engagement.

page 78
Student selections will vary. Check to see that a variety of forms have been used to express the same idea.

pages 79-80-81
Questions, research, and writing will vary. Check student writing for clear, interesting answers to the question, use of reliable information, and correct citations.

pages 82-83
1. *pretty-patterned purples paint; sharp crimson spikes shoot; glistening golds glitter, blasts of blues burst into the blackness; fuchsia fragments fling; chasing after twinkling chartreuse; silence is split*
2. *shoot, burst, twinkling, split, cracks, pops, roar, clatter*
3. Lines that begin *And pretty-patterned purples; Fuchsia fragments fling themselves; Yellows sparkle; To claw at the skies*
4. *spikes shoot like arrows*
5. The layout looks like fireworks and suggests energy and movement.
6. Answers will vary.
Check student paragraphs, looking for a clear, well-written answer to the question and effective use of direct quotes.

page 84
Summaries will vary. Check to see that they flow smoothly, make sense, and summarize the main points.

Speaking and Listening (pages 86-98)

pages 86-89
Check to see that students have adequately completed the Prepare; Listen, Respect, Respond; and Reflect parts of the Collaborator's Guide.

pages 90-94
Check students'

Presentation Response Forms completed in response to the listening task on page 92, as well as the I Hear You questions and the Argumentative Speech Reflection. Look for complete, thoughtful answers that indicate careful listening.

pages 95-97

Review students' preparation notes and reflections for their own speeches. Look for complete and thoughtful answers. Apply standards SL.7.4-6 in listening to their interview/speeches.

page 98

Review student evaluations of each other's speeches to see that comments and suggestions support the numerical ratings.

Language (pages 100-126)

page 100

A. 1. *conducting the interview* (used to describe the noun *reporter*); *in this location* (used as an adverb to modify the verb *worked*)

2. *Learning to talk to animals* (used as the subject of the sentence); *in night school* (used as an adverb to modify the verb *studies*)

3. *Those fish with the long bodies, huge jaws, and sharp teeth* (used to identify the subject of the sentence *barracudas*); *with the long bodies, huge jaws, and sharp teeth* (used to modify the noun *fish*)

4. *preying on the other sea creatures* (used to modify the noun *barracuda*); *on the other sea creatures* (used to modify the verb *preying*); *of the*

sea (used to modify the noun *tiger*)

B. Sentences will vary. Check to see that they include accurately identified phrases.

page 101

A. 1. *which was caught up in a storm* (used as an adjective to modify the noun *whale*)

2. *A crowd gathered around the whale* (independent clause); *the chance that the whale might perish on the beach* (used as the object of the preposition *about*).

3. *whoever was on the beach* (used as indirect object of the verb *enlisted*)

4. *Because the whale's survival depended on staying hydrated* (used to modify the verb *kept*); *biologists kept the animal wet as they examined it* (independent clause)

5. *who encouraged the whale and helped keep her wet* (used to modify the noun *people*)

6. *That the whale tipped her tail toward the beach* (used as the subject of the sentence)

B. 7 and 8. Sentences will vary. Check to see that students have added clauses fitting the directed requirements.

page 102

1. CX
2. C
3. CC
4. CX
5. S
6. C
7. CX
8. CX
9. S
10. CX
11. S

page 103

Sentences will vary. Check to see that student has written sentences to match the sentence-type labels.

page 104

Answers may vary somewhat. Here are some possible rearrangements.

1. A dolphin tickled me while I was dangling my feet in the ocean.

2. The swimmers were shocked to see a fin jutting out of the sea.

3. When the crab poked its head in the sand, I noticed its monstrous claws.

4. The ocean looked very peaceful as I rode horseback along the beach.

5. Why did you buy unwrapped saltwater taffy at that store?

6. A big wave unexpectedly wiped out the sand castle Joe had built.

7. At least ten times this week, my mother told me to put on sunscreen.

8. With great care, I repaired the raft that was punctured by the shark.

page 105

Answers may vary somewhat. Here are some possible rearrangements.

1. The surfer in her wet suit spotted a shark.

2. Sam joined Brett and me for a snack at our campfire.

3. Three dolphins teased Alonzo while he was paddling his board.

4. When we were lying on the raft, the sun burned us badly.

5. The swimmer's blue goggles were swept away by a wave.

6. By mistake, Sophie dropped the

sandwich she was carrying onto the sand.

7. The monster wave roared behind me when I was standing on the surfboard.

8. The icy lemonade called out to me when I was hot and tired from a jog on the beach.

9. The boys served s'mores oozing with melted chocolate to their friends.

page 106

Reading from the lower left corner of the page and following the wave, insert commas after *coming, Todd, Kate, Oh, Beach, California, formidable, Well, him, seems, air, forward, itself, crunchy, battered, shaken, terrified, Hey, guys, friends, me, suit, realized, wicked.*

page 107

Commas are needed on the following signs:
ENJOY OUR FUN, FRIENDLY ATMOSPHERE
WE'RE JUST A SHORT, SCENIC DRIVE FROM DOWNTOWN
WE SPECIALIZE IN RED, WHITE, AND BLUE ACCESSORIES
FIND NEW, USED, AND REFURBISHED BOARDS
OUR HELPFUL, KNOWLEDGABLE STAFF IS HERE FOR YOU
In the letter, delete commas after *fancy* and *beach*.

page 108

I. Misspelled or misused words spelled correctly: certain, advice, which, obvious, reel, losing, accepted, attitude, tired, speech, inducted

II. 1. through, through
2. whether, weather
3. prosecute
4. a lot
5. angel
6. commas
7. inflict
8. incredible

page 109

1. beautiful
2. received
3. generous
4. *OK*
5. compliments
6. exclaimed
7. uncontrollable
8. pleasant
9. *OK*
10. unfortunately
11. *OK*
12. truly
13. probably
14. remember
Correction in speech balloon: noticed

page 110

Letters will vary. Check to see that the letter has good word choice, eliminates redundancies, flows well, and makes sense.

page 111

1. monumental
2. turbulent
3. elude
4. stymied
5. notorious
6. adverse
7. credulous
8. quarrelsome
9. flouting
10. obligated
11. nadir
12. loath

page 112

Student guesses may vary somewhat. Here are some possibilities:
1. generosity
2. lack
3. gently encourage
4. intruders
5. dishonest
6. rowdy, wild
7. rolling
8. praise

Copyright © 2014 World Book, Inc./ Incentive Publications, Chicago, IL

page 113
1. augment
2. absconded
3. scrutinize
4. tortuous
5. quell
6. superfluous
7. pique
8. cognizant
9. acrid
10. voracious

page 114
1. L
2. F
3. M
4. O
5. N
6. B
7. E, C
8. D
9. K
10. G

page 115
1. seascape or aquascape
2. fragment
3. revolve
4. final
5. cooperate
6. transportable
7. aerospace
8. sonic
9. verbalize
10. mariner
11. geoscience
12. athletic
13. submarine
14. thermal
15. autograph
16. wooden

page 116
Words may vary; possibilities include words below. Check for accurate meanings.
1. contortionist, distort, extort, torture
2. illuminate, luminescence, luminous
3. hypothermia, thermos, thermostat, endothermic, thermometer, thermal

4. vision, visor, supervise, visible, visibility
5. telegraph, telephone, telecast, telescope
6. rotate, rotisserie, rotary
7. enflame, flammable, flamboyant, inflammatory
8. asteroid, astronaut, astronomy
9. populate, overpopulate, popularity, unpopular, populous, population
10. pedestrian, pedal, expedite, biped
11. location, allocate, relocate, local
12. culpable, culprit
13. nature, national, neonatal, native
14. section, dissect, sector
15. annual, anniversary
16. gyroscope, gyrate

page 117
Answers may vary. Listen to student reasons for their choices. Allow any reasonable answers.
1. no
2. possibly
3. yes
4. no
5. no
6. yes
7. yes
8. no
9. yes
10. no
11. possibly (would be a funny feat)
12. no
13. no (or possibly)
14. yes, no, or possibly
15. no
16. yes
17. yes
18. no

page 118
1. in the ocean
2. on a roast beef
3. in a nerve cell

4. in your ear
5. on a leaf
6. in outer space
7. on a shelf
8. around a leg
9. around the sun
10. at a church
11. on your face
12. in a drama
13. swimming in the sea
14. in your nose
15. on a cathedral
16. in a speech
17. in a library
18. in an orchestra

page 119
Answers will vary. Student answers should show understanding of the word meaning.
1. A bad disposition could lead you to annoy or provoke the shark and this could be dangerous.
2. A jellyfish might sting your nose (proboscis).
3. It's unsafe to ski behind a boat with a sleeping driver.
4. Anemones can sting you. Sea life is healthier if you leave plants and animals alone.
5. Jodhpurs are wide and heavy. They'd bog you down in water.
6. You don't want a lifeguard who has a fear of water!
7. With little seaweed, the water is clearer, and you won't get tangled.
8. Wandering into dark waters would inhibit you from seeing the manta.
9. An inept instructor is incompetent!
10. A maelstrom will toss your boat—maybe sink it.
11. When sea lions fight, you're safer to stay

out of the way.
12. Turbulent waters are rough and dangerous.

page 120
Answers will vary. Accept answers that convey the meaning of the idiom. In the drawings, look for visual representation of literal meanings.
1. You're bothered about something.
2. He believed every word of my story.
3. She's doing too much at once.
4. This information is from the person who really knows.
5. Mom is in trouble.
6. I know she has secrets that she's hiding.
7. Once again, she has said something foolish or embarrassing.
8. You've been caught; you're in trouble.
9. I'll use my influence to get you a ticket.
10. I took a risk for her when she needed help.

page 121
Idioms in the story: good egg, blew my mind, bite the bullet, go for it, got cold feet, backed out, chickening out, under the gun, sweating bullets, get this group off my back, shaking in my boots, my heart in my throat, feeling like a million bucks, more fun than a barrel of monkeys.
Student stories will vary. Check to see that several figures of speech have been used appropriately.

page 122
1. hypnotize
2. ineptness
3. article
4. respiration
5. lazy

6. calm
7. toxin
8. detective
9. soup
10. charlatan

page 123
1. S, waiver
2. W, conductor
3. R, climb
4. D, blizzard
5. F, cleanse
6. L, opera
7. A, greed
8. C, cappuccino

page 124
Answers will vary. Look for answers that use the concept of connotation to show the broader impressions, images, and ideas communicated by the words.

page 125
Answers will vary. Look for answers that demonstrate student understanding of the way connotation relates to words chosen in particular situations and the way that each word switch affects the meaning and impact on the reader.

page 126
periodic: happening or recurring at intervals
gravitational pull: the pull of gravity toward something
cycles: a complete series of events that is repeated
high tide: the time when the water reaches its highest level; happens twice a day
low tide: the time when the water reaches its lowest level; happens twice a day
tidal currents: the water flow (current) caused by the tides

Copyright © 2014 World Book, Inc./ Incentive Publications, Chicago, IL